Praise for *Make Change Work*

"I could rename this book, *How Tulips, Dodo Birds, and Coyotes Changed the Way I Think about Change*. Interested now? You should be. This book is the most fascinating, practical book about dealing with change I've ever read."

—Larry Winget
Television personality and best-selling author of
*Grow a Pair: How to Stop Being a Victim and
Take Back Your Life, Your Business, and Your Sanity*

"*Make Change Work* is the best book I have read on the real inner workings of change. It could have easily been called *The Future Belongs to the Coyote*. Pennington does a great job of equating the emotional side of change with the pragmatic, 'let's get it done' side. Lessons for the future rest on these pages, no matter how many change scenarios we might have dealt with as managers."

—Gary Nelon
Chairman, First Texas Bancorp

"The highest praise I can give a book: 'You will use it.' Randy Pennington has written an extraordinary book about change (and leadership, and culture, and execution, and more) that you won't just enjoy reading; you will use the ideas in it the second you put it down. From his thoughts on 'what's on top of your refrigerator' to 'unpacking the baggage,' you'll be thinking 'I can do that' and 'We have to do that' and 'Why haven't we done that?' and then you'll do it. Let me say it flat out, Randy Pennington is the best business writer I know, and this book will significantly impact and improve the way you do business."

—Joe Calloway
Author, *Be the Best at What Matters Most*

"Randy worked with our global Human Resources team and his practical, high energy approach provided a catalyst for us to stop waiting for results and culture to happen and take personal ownership. His latest book, *Make Change Work,* lays a simple path from the strategy to tactics for change. Randy teaches leaders to attack change not as a process to manage but as a way of operating that is reinforced by good habits and constant reminders that we celebrate and reward people for taking on change that delivers results."

—**Susan Kelliher**
SVP Human Resources,
Albemarle Corporation

"The most challenging aspect of successfully managing change is providing leadership to the individuals in your organization who must buy into your vision. *Make Change Work* provides real world, practical ideas for leading change—understanding that in order for organizations to change, the people in those organizations must change. Randy Pennington brings the importance of leadership into sharp focus and provides strategies you can use immediately to make change work."

—**Chris Korst**
Executive Vice President, Operations Rent-A-Center

"In order to make change work, we have to change the way we work. Period. Randy Pennington takes you on a journey to not only change but also how to lead transformation."

—**Brian Solis**
Author, *What's the Future of Business* (WTF);
Principal Analyst at Altimeter Group

"Randy Pennington skillfully charts out the path to becoming a successful leader in an ever-changing world. His analysis and expertise provide valuable advice that can be adapted to all organizations and businesses."

—**Dr. Nido Qubein**
President, High Point University;
Chairman, Great Harvest Bread Co.

"Innovative. Insightful. Engaging. Actionable. Most business books I read have one or two of those qualities—but, Randy Pennington's new *Make Change Work* is an elite effort that captures all four. His thoughts on change WILL truly change—and *enhance*—your business and career. Buy it . . . read it . . . and make change work for YOU!"

—**Scott McKain**
Author, *Create Distinction*

"My legal department wants everyone to know that my opinion doesn't represent the official view of the company, but I love this book. Randy Pennington lays out a clear case for why making change work is a competitive advantage for your company, and then he shows you exactly what must be done to execute that strategy. Randy knows what works. His experience is front and center in this excellent book."

—**Karen Klein**
Senior Vice President, Transamerica
Life Insurance Company

"This isn't just another book about change; it is a manual written by a change leader with vast experience. Pennington's deep work with a multitude of clients has enabled him to create a blueprint you can use to make change work in your business. Not only is it a good read, it produces results."

—**Mark Sanborn**
Best-selling author,
The Fred Factor and *Fred 2.0*

"*Make Change Work* is that rare book that combines strategic insights and direction with practical how-to ideas for addressing specific challenges. This book will help leaders at every level be more effective at driving change and delivering results."

—**Mark Rieck**
Executive Vice President,
International Right of Way Association

"Filled with truths for ensuring you remain relevant in an ever changing environment, Pennington has masterfully captured his years of coaching and consulting in a concise, thought-provoking commentary on the challenges and solutions for successfully leading change."

—**Terry Pankratz**
Vice President for Budget & Finance,
University of Texas at Dallas

"Leadership, by definition, is about change—making the case, preparing people, marshaling resources, producing desired outcomes, and making it stick. *Make Change Work* offers both foundational principles and practical playbook ideas to ensure success in the change journey. And it is written in a conversational, storytelling, and sometimes humorous style making it accessible and quite effective for executives and managers at all levels. *Make Change Work* is an invaluable read for anyone who aspires to lead."

—Henry S. Givray
President & CEO, SmithBucklin Corporation

"Randy Pennington has articulated, in one book, the essentials of implementing real and lasting change. His approach is easy to understand. The methodologies and tools provided can readily be used or adapted to any organization. I recommend it to anyone facing changes in their work environment, and, I think, that includes all of us."

—Michael Di Paolo
Associate Vice Chancellor and CIO,
University of North Texas System

"Make Change Work is that rare business book that tells you what it takes to stay relevant and deliver results to the customers you serve *and* shows you how to actually execute that change. Every member of your team should read and apply the lessons from this book. It could mean the difference between thriving and extinction."

—David DuBois, CAE, CMP, FASAE, CTA
President and CEO, International
Association of Exhibitions and Events

"Dynamite does indeed come in small packages. *Make Change Work* will explode so many myths about how and why change works. Randy Pennington has spent decades teaching leaders how to be better by changing the culture of their organizations. He delivers a culture change toolkit in his latest, and as usual, easy-reading book. It doesn't matter if you are a manager expected to implement change or a person who feels intimidated by the change seeming to engulf you, this book will build your confidence to embrace and implement change. Treat yourself to this enlightening book. I have been leading change in government organizations for 40 years. I am a better change agent because I did."

—Leonard Martin
City Manager, City of Carrollton, Texas

"Randy Pennington has written the best book I have read on the subject of change. Most books talk about why change is needed; few tell how to tackle it and make it work for you. This book is packed with practical and actionable strategies on how to actually deal with change and how to lead it. His systematic approach will make a difference in your life and your organization. Simply put: Read this and learn to love change."

—Lisa Ford
Author, *Exceptional Customer Service*

"We're entering the period of the most accelerated change in human history. The biggest challenge for entrepreneurs will be how to get in front of it and make it work. Fortunately Randy Pennington just wrote a book on how to do just that. If you are ready to become a change leader, read it."

—Randy Gage
Author of the *New York Times*
best seller, *Risky Is the New Safe*

"I read more than 100 business books a year and *Make Change Work* is now my absolute favorite on dealing effectively with change. Randy delivers super ideas, sage advice, and plenty of solid tools, all while keeping it fun and entertaining. To survive in the 'new normal' you MUST develop Nimblocity (being nimble with velocity), and *Make Change Work* is your handbook! This is a book your entire team should read!"

—John Spence
One of the top 100 business thought leaders in America

"Randy Pennington's new book, *Make Change Work*, is a must-read, innovative approach to dealing with the dynamics of change! If you want to learn how to be a change leader, make this strategic investment in your future. This book will heighten your awareness, give you bulleted action lists, and provide benefits you don't want to be deprived of, so get it today and profit from it tomorrow!"

—Don Hutson
Coauthor of the #*1 New York Times* best seller,
The One Minute Entrepreneur, CEO of US Learning

"Managing and leading change at every level in the organization is one of the most critical aspects to master, in order to grow your career and business, today and in the future. Randy Pennington has put together a book with realistic examples, expectations, and actionable items that deal with the world of change. *Make Change Work* is a great road map and easy to apply book that will allow you to maximize your cultural competitive advantage and adapt to any challenge."

—Chris Moses
VP Total Rewards and Performance
Systems, Albemarle Corporation

"The most well written book about change and how to use it to your benefit. In an uncertain world, the one thing we are certain of is change. As I studied Randy's words, he has outlined the ways to embrace this change within your organization and personal life and to act upon it. Unlike most authors, Pennington has done years of research about what distinguishes great companies and leaders that have thrived in challenging and unstable environments. With tips, calls to action, and the harsh reality of change, Randy really teaches you the tools you need to succeed in the ever-so-turbulent times of change."

—Chad Hymas
Author, *Doing What Must Be Done*

MAKE CHANGE WORK

MAKE CHANGE WORK

Staying Nimble, Relevant, and
Engaged in a World of
Constant Change

RANDY PENNINGTON

WILEY

Library of Congress Cataloging-in-Publication Data:

Pennington, Randy.
   Make change Work: Staying Nimble, Relevant, and Engaged in a World of Constant
change/Randy Pennington.
     Includes index.
   ISBN: 978-1-118-61746-5 (cloth); ISBN: 978-1-118-72287-9 (ebk);
   ISBN: 978-1-118-72233-6 (ebk)
     1. Organizational change.   2. Organizational effectiveness.   I. Title.
  HD58.8
  658.4'06–dc23

                 2013016102

Printed in the United States of America
10 9 8 7 6 5 4 3 2 1

To Mary, who never asked me to change and
encouraged me to continually adapt.
And to the leaders who are making change work.

CONTENTS

Preface   *xv*
Acknowledgments   *xix*

Part I   **The Realities of Change**   **1**
Chapter 1   The New Normal   3
Chapter 2   Faster, Better, Cheaper, Friendlier   13
Chapter 3   Good Change, Bad Change   21
Chapter 4   Dodos and Coyotes: Only the Nimble Survive   33

Part II   **Becoming a Change Leader: The Tactical**
                Side of Change   **41**
Chapter 5   What Change Leaders Do   43
Chapter 6   Buy-In: Where Change Legends Are Made   51
Chapter 7   Go First   59
Chapter 8   Change Change   67
Chapter 9   Generate Creative Tension   75
Chapter 10   Connect with People Where They Are   85
Chapter 11   Involve Early and Often   95
Chapter 12   Use Resistance as Your Friend   103

Part III   **Change Challenges**   **113**
Chapter 13   When Change Isn't a Choice   115
Chapter 14   Change Your Culture and Change Your Results   125
Chapter 15   Stop Spineating   135

Part IV   **The Wrap-Up**   **143**
Chapter 16   The Future and Change   145

Notes   *153*
About the Author   *157*
Index   *159*

PREFACE

The difference between winning and losing is how the men and women of our company view change as it comes at them.

—Jack Welch
Former chief executive officer,
General Electric

Another book about change? Really? The thousands of other books on the subject aren't enough?

I'm with you.

My iceberg has moved. My cheese has melted, and I don't need to hear another message that changes are coming and I need to get on board.

And yet we are confronted with this reality: Most of our efforts to make change work don't work as well as we had hoped . . . or even at all.

Need proof?

Research published by John Kotter[1] in 1995 stated that 70 percent of change efforts fail to achieve their desired goal. Since that time, there has been an explosion in books, articles, training videos, seminars, and speeches about change.

So what impact did we achieve from all of our focus on change?

In 2013, 18 years after Kotter's study, every indication is that the vast majority of change efforts—as high as 70 percent by some reports—fail to achieve their desired goal.

That's right. There has been basically a whopping 0 percent improvement in our collective ability to effectively initiate and implement change.

We can now conclude that all of our attention and focus on change hasn't really changed our ability to successfully implement change in organizations.

But you knew that already. Think of all the changes you have experienced within the organizations for which you have worked. Don't you think we would be better at it by now?

CHANGE IS IMPORTANT

My favorite *Far Side* comic of all time features a dinosaur standing behind a lectern in front of a room of other dinosaurs. The caption reads, "The picture is pretty bleak, gentlemen. The world's climate is changing, the mammals are taking over, and we all have a brain about the size of a walnut."

Relentless competition, advancing technology, and the struggle to remain relevant have made the ability to change a matter of survival for some industries and professions.

There is another story to be told, however. The ability to make change work is a strategic advantage.

Companies that can quickly identify, anticipate, and adapt to changing customer needs and wants are the winners in a world where the competitive landscape changes overnight. Leaders with the ability to build a nimble team that is engaged and focused on continually getting better will see their opportunities expand.

You can't do what you need to do and be what you need to be as a leader unless you can make change work.

LET'S TALK ABOUT YOU

You are reading this book for one of three reasons:

1. You saw the title and were intrigued. You may be struggling with a change that needs to be made right now. You know that your team, department, and company need to be better at making change work if you hope to remain relevant and competitive in the marketplace. You often feel overwhelmed by the amount of change that is coming at you and the speed at which it arrives. You are looking for answers—even just one or two ideas—that will help you be more effective.

2. Your boss or company gave you this book and told you to read it. Their reasons are probably related to the previous point, but that doesn't change the fact that this book is an imposed

assignment rather than the book you chose to pick up for your after-hours consumption.

3. You know me, are related to me, or have read one of my previous books. You may be interested to see what is on my mind, like my writing style, or feel obligated to know what I have said in case you run into me and I ask, "So, how did you like the book?"

WHAT YOU WILL FIND

This book is written for the leader who wants to make change work. It shares the lessons I've learned in over 20 years of helping leaders and organizations change. Much of that work—or at least something more than 30 percent—has been successful. Some of it has not. I have made a substantial part of my living helping organizations of all shapes and sizes implement change. I like to think the fact that they keep asking me for help means that I'm doing a few things correctly.

And there is something for the rest of you, too.

First, this book is short. It is written in small digestible chunks that will make it less painful for those being forced to read it and easier to grab relevant bites for those of you who want to make me feel good when I run into you.

Second, I hope you can already see that I am very passionate about the importance of actually making change work *and* that I want to make this at least a little entertaining. My goal is to make this a conversation, and like any conversation, there will be opportunities to interject a degree of levity.

HOW THE BOOK WORKS

The book is presented in four parts.

- Part I is about the strategic side of change. It talks about the pace and scope of change today. It also shares ideas about why change doesn't work, defines what good change looks like in today's organizations, and provides an interesting comparison of dodos and coyotes. These animals, I believe, represent the best and worst characteristics of making change work today.

- Part II is about becoming a change leader. It is the more tactical side. You will learn seven strategies and competencies for increasing the effectiveness of your change efforts. We won't devote time to traditional change management principles of project management. There are many excellent resources for doing that.
- Part III addresses the specific challenges that present themselves when change isn't a choice (such as when a company downsizes or merges with another company) and you want to change your organization's culture. Of all the changes that you will be asked to implement, our experience shows that these are the most difficult. You will also learn about how destructive stimulus-response loops prevent individuals and organizations from effectively responding to change.
- Part IV looks to the future. The Greek philosopher Heraclitus said, "There is nothing permanent except change." The pace and scope of change will only increase.

Each of the chapters contains bulleted action lists and opportunities to work on the application of the principles and strategies. Throughout the book you will see the names of clients and case studies. When you see a first and last name, it is the actual person. When you see only a first name, the example has been sanitized so that it will not embarrass the individual involved.

THE BIG IDEA

Ross Perot, founder of EDS and Perot Systems and former candidate for US president, famously said: "You manage data and things. You lead people."

Change—when it is done well—is a competitive advantage that allows you to be more nimble and relevant in the marketplace.

Too often, we have treated people like data and things to be managed rather than as human beings with dreams, aspirations, and choices. We won't make change work until we embrace the difference as an opportunity to make our organizations, our communities, and our lives better.

Let's get started.

ACKNOWLEDGMENTS

Implementing and executing change is both science and art. It's sociologic, psychological, and organizational principles and steps can be learned through study. The art of change is learned through experience. I have been extremely fortunate to work on change initiatives of all shapes and sizes—from relatively straightforward policy changes to complex cultural transformations—in a wide range of public and private sector organizations. This, as I was recently reminded by a client, is not my first rodeo. And each of these experiences has taught me the valuable lesson that every bull is different.

So to every one of those clients, thank you for trusting me to help you reach your goals.

For me, a book requires space, support, and motivation. My wife and business partner Mary willingly provided the space for me to write on weekends when it would have been nice to do something more fun. Dr. Jack Pennington, my brother, challenged me to think more deeply about how people respond to change. I appreciate the push.

The team at John Wiley & Sons, Inc., gave me the support and motivation to get this book off the ground and completed. Thank you to Shannon Vargo, Tiffany Colon, Susan Moran, and the entire production team. Matt Holt, you are a great book guy with excellent taste in music and bourbon. You were right about the cover.

I owe a huge thank you to my buddies in the business. You know who you are. You challenge me to live up to your standard, put up with my crap; and you get it.

And finally, thank you for reading this book. There are a lot of changes that need to take place in our world, and you have the guts to step up and lead them.

Part I

THE REALITIES
OF CHANGE

Chapter 1

THE NEW NORMAL

There is nothing permanent except change.

—Heraclitus

WHEN WILL THINGS RETURN TO NORMAL?

James was in a bind. His heating and air-conditioning business had grown along with the housing boom. He had expanded his business on the assumption that low interest rates and easy-to-obtain mortgages would keep his business growing until he could reach his goal of employing five crews and paying off his debt. At that point, his business would be sustainable even if there was an economic slowdown.

The collapse of the housing bubble caught James completely off guard.

"When will things get back to normal?" he asked during a presentation.

It was a question I had received numerous times since the economic meltdown of 2008. Most people—like James—want to know when the job market will bounce back, when the economy will return to something close to sustained growth, when the uncertainty about our future will subside, or when the rate of change will slow to a more manageable pace.

The answer they want is a timetable for returning to stable markets, low unemployment, and customers who buy their products and services. They hope for a world that is similar to the one in which they knew how to compete and succeed.

My answer is always the same and often unpopular: What if this is it? What if instability, rapid change, and uncertainty about things out of your control are the new normal? And, what if I'm wrong and things bounce back quickly? If you can succeed now, you will crush it then.

Unfortunately for James, I wasn't wrong.

PERSPECTIVE FROM THE IRON LADY

"The world has changed forever."

Those words flooded the media in the days and weeks following the terrorist attacks on the United States on September 11, 2001. Many of the conferences at which I was scheduled to speak cancelled during that time, but one did not. The closing speaker was Lady Margaret Thatcher.

Lady Thatcher, the longest-serving prime minister in Great Britain's storied history, had survived World War II as a little girl. She had experienced the cold war and numerous terrorist bombings in her own country during the 1970s and 1980s. She had led her country through dramatic change. She, as much as anyone in the world, had the perspective to make sense of the attacks on the United States.

Her words are as relevant today as they were then: "The world has stayed the same. It is just that our illusions have been stripped away."

REFRAMING OUR ILLUSIONS

Humans have a tendency to believe that their initial experience with a situation is the first time that it has occurred. Every change that makes you nervous, uncertain, and sometimes a little crazy has occurred in some form before.

New technology has always been a disruptive and beneficial force in how people work and live. The folk legend John Henry was a steel-driving man who raced against the steam-powered hammer that revolutionized the building of the railroads. The telegraph opened a new era of communication that created new jobs while making others unnecessary. Business has always looked for ways to do things faster, better, cheaper, or friendlier, and technology has played a major role. Why would that be different today?

Globalization has existed since the beginning of time. Overland trade routes between western Asia, the Mediterranean region, and China date to the second millennium BCE. The travel took longer and was much more precarious, but it brought imports, exports, new jobs, and competition for existing jobs among countries and individuals. The opportunities and threats of globalization today are the logical extension of a history of expansion into new markets to sell, purchase, and produce goods and services.

The Dutch Tulip Bubble of 1637 shares an eerily similar feeling to the banking and mortgage crisis of 2008. Tulips were the speculative currency of the time in Holland. Fortunes were made and lost daily as tulip traders speculated on what appeared to be an investment that would only increase in price. Then someone didn't show up to pay for his tulips. Widespread panic ensued. Tulip prices plunged to virtually nothing, and the Netherlands was forced into a depression that lasted years.

Wars have been waged (formally and informally) forever. American political scientist Quincy Wright wrote: "Change in any particular force, trend, movement, or policy may at one time make for war, but under other conditions a similar change may make for peace." In other words, the world is a very unstable place because humans act in their own interests rather than looking at what is best for their country or the world.

I SHOULD HAVE PAID ATTENTION

How many times have you said to yourself, "If I had only known . . . "?

- If I had only known that I would be doing business with people in other countries, I would have paid more attention in my language classes in school.
- If I had only known that entering information on a keyboard would be an important part of my life, I would have taken a typing class.
- If I had only known about the Dutch Tulip Bubble of 1637, I might not have lost all that money in the bursting of the dot-com bubble or the housing bubble.
- If I had only known that I would actually need my hearing, I wouldn't have played music so loud when I was a teenager. (Okay. That's not true. My parents told me to turn it down, and I didn't. How about you?)

The list is endless.

History repeating itself doesn't make us feel any better as we are experiencing it for ourselves. In fact, it can make us feel stupid and out of touch.

But before you get too angry or frustrated, take comfort in knowing two things:

1. You are not alone. Most people and organizations miss the big changes that affect their lives until it is too late to do anything other than play catch up.
2. There are some aspects of this change that make the new normal different.

MOORE'S LAW AFFECTS EVERYTHING

You have probably heard of Moore's law. In case you haven't, here is the overview:

> Gordon Moore, cofounder of technology giant Intel, wrote in 1965 that the number of transistors that could be placed on an integrated circuit doubles approximately every two years while the production cost moves in the opposite direction. What is now called Moore's law was based on his observations about chip development from 1958 (the creation of the first integrated circuit) until 1965, and it explains why it now costs a few hundred dollars to purchase a laptop computer that has more power than the largest mainframe machines of just a few decades back.

Most important for you, 50-plus years of Moore's law has created exponential growth in the impact of technology to change your world and your work. And that change affects everything: globalization, economics, how wars are waged and fought, how work is accomplished, how we communicate, and our ability to keep up with everything that might affect our lives.

Connected financial markets didn't create the bad decisions that fueled the global financial meltdown and sovereign debt problems of 2008 to 2009. They simply allowed more banks in more countries to share and be harmed by the risks.

Social media didn't create the Arab Spring. It simply allowed people to more effectively organize and communicate their message.

Today's technology did not create terrorists or rebels. It simply removed any illusion from our psyche that any single place or people are safe.

WE LIVE IN AN OCEAN NOT A POND

The scariest change on the horizon is the one that you don't see coming until it hits you. There were people who saw the ability of technology to take the globalization of work to a new level just as there were those who saw the Great Recession and health care reform and computing in the cloud on the horizon.

What separates them from the rest of us is that we focus on the pond in which we live. They look for trends in the ocean.

An old French children's riddle is a great way to think about the realities of change today. It goes like this:

> A pond has one lily pad in it today. The number of lily pads in the pond doubles every day, and on day 30 the pond is completely full. On what day is the pond half full of lily pads?

Day 29 is a convenient way to describe the overwhelming power of exponential growth demonstrated by Moore's law. But it misses an important point: The pond in the lily pad riddle is a fixed size. Day 30 assumes no more capacity and then you are done.

That's not the way it works when it comes to change today. You may feel like you are at day 29½, with a finite capacity for absorbing more change, but the rest of the world hasn't received or accepted that message. In the real world, the pond is really an ocean with unlimited capacity to expand.

Those who thrive in today's hyper-change environment see further and adapt quicker. The result is that they are more relevant to their customers, engaged in staying ahead of the change and nimble when placed in a position to react.

CHANGE LEADER ACTION LIST

All change creates moments of instability and anxiety. Substantial change that comes at you in waves can either make you bold or make you timid.

(continued)

(*continued*)

Now is not the time to be timid. Timid companies don't anticipate the future. Timid people don't invest in themselves or take the actions that enable them to quickly adapt.

Here are three action items you can take to increase your opportunity to thrive in the midst of the new realities of change.

1. Focus on Value Given and Value Received

In uncertain financial times, investors run toward value. Your customers do the same thing. Your challenge is to add so much value that doing business with you takes away any anxiety or fear they may have. You must be crystal clear about the return on their investment you will deliver. How can you make it faster, better, cheaper, or friendlier?

This principle also applies to your career. Your employer will base decisions on the value you provide for the investment the company is making. If you aren't creating more value than the cost of keeping you, why should the company bother?

2. Strategically Invest in Your Future

The biggest threat most of us face is relevancy. People who purchase your product or service are asking, "Why you? Why now? What makes you relevant?"

Employers who are deciding to hire you or even keep you on the payroll are asking the same questions.

Now is the time to strategically invest in the areas that will make you successful five years from now while continuing to add value today. That could mean investing in a new product, service, or piece of equipment. Or it could mean learning a new skill. The best in every field of endeavor actively manage their futures. This is more important today than ever before.

3. Prepare for the Worst and Look for the Best

Long-term anxiety and instability breed a lack of confidence. And that lack of confidence closes our minds to opportunity.

The Great Depression of the 1930s saw the demise of many companies, but it also gave us companies such as Motorola, Texas Instruments, Hewlett-Packard, and Converse.

The same will be true of today. Fifty years from now, we'll look back on this time as the crucible that spawned legendary brands and businesses.

I'm a realist. There are a number of factors that affect your success. The only one you can control is what you do to see further and adapt faster than the other guy.

Chapter 2

FASTER, BETTER, CHEAPER, FRIENDLIER

Even if you are on the right track, you'll get run over if you just sit there.

—Will Rogers

A HARD DOSE OF REALITY

"There is a rumor going around that if this doesn't work, we'll go back to the way we did things before."

Marcus, the senior leader in charge of implementing the change to a shared services organization, smiled and said, "I've heard that rumor, too."

A flash of hopeful anticipation enveloped the room as employees hoped to hear that a retreat was possible if this change didn't work.

"And I can tell you," Marcus continued, "that's not going to happen. We aren't going back. If we don't get this right, they will find people who will. We will either be outsourced or replaced."

BURN THE BOATS—THE CUSTOMERS ARE IN CHARGE

Listening to my client's response reminded me of the ancient Greek army commanders when they landed on an enemy shore. Their first order was to burn the boats as a physical sign that they weren't going back.

Your customers—both external and internal—are in charge. They know that a viable alternative to your product or service is a phone call or mouse click away. Technology and globalization have given them the power for which they have always longed, and they aren't giving it back.

They want it faster, better, cheaper, and/or friendlier. You either meet those expectations or run the risk that they will find someone or some third party who will.

TOUGH CUSTOMERS—TOUGH QUESTIONS

You don't need me to tell you that customers are tougher to please and more demanding. You can prove it for yourself.

Joe Calloway, author of the book *Becoming a Category of One,* says, "There's a new sheriff in town. It's the customer."[1]

He proves it by asking readers to answer 10 questions about their own experiences. I liked them so much that I asked for permission to share them with you. Read them and remember—every one of your customers is thinking about you when they answer these questions.

1. Are you a tougher customer than you were five years ago?
2. Are you a more informed and more educated buyer than you were five years ago?
3. Are you more likely to complain on the spot if you experience a problem?
4. Do you demand better service than you used to?
5. If you do not receive the service you want, are you more likely to fire that business and never come back?
6. Are you more likely today to take action, such as writing or calling a company's management with a complaint?
7. Do you tell more people today about companies that you have experienced problems with?
8. Do you take "no" for an answer, or are you more likely to go up the chain of command until you get satisfaction?
9. Do you demand more value today than ever before for every dollar that you spend?
10. Do you feel that you have choices about the people you do business with and that you will exercise those choices in a heartbeat if you don't get the service you want?[2]

HOW CUSTOMERS EVALUATE YOUR EFFORTS

We are evaluated against the best—not the average example—of our customers' experience. For me, that means you are evaluated against Carl when it comes to Web design and technology services.

Carl Thomas, owner of P.R. Inc., has been our go-to guy for web and materials design for years. We love Carl because he's smart, he's easy to do business with, and he gets us. We also love the fact that we can meet with Carl this morning and have a prototype back the next morning that requires very little change.

Carl's secret weapon is Claude—a very talented developer who lives in Romania. I give something to Carl, and Claude is hard at work while I am asleep.

I could demand that Carl use a local developer, and I am sure he could come up with someone to do my work. But I don't really care.

I want it faster, better, cheaper, and friendlier. Carl and Claude give that to me. I appreciate it, will continue to do business with them, and, most important, evaluate every service provider with whom I do business based on my experience with them. You do it, too. So do your customers.

TOOLS THAT ACCELERATE

Imagine that you work on the framing crew in the residential construction business. You probably felt comfortable and secure as long as the handful of crews competing for work were all using the same tools, operating on the same schedule, and charging the same rates.

But what happens when the crew next to you uses a heavy-duty pneumatic air hammer while you continue with your trusted 16-ounce claw hammer? What happens if the other crew can work longer hours or for lower wages.

Even scarier, what happens if the general contractor decides to purchase technology that does your work faster, cheaper, or better without you?

That metaphor applied to your industry is the reality of faster, better, cheaper, and friendlier. Today's success proves that you were once right.

There are new tools on the horizon that will make what is cutting edge today feel antiquated in a matter of months or years. These tools will have the ability to render business models obsolete, empower companies around the world to compete with those around the corner, and give individuals an immediate global voice to shape the future of society.

You are signing on to a never-ending effort, not a one-time event. Get ready. Faster, better, cheaper, and friendlier are about to push you to places we've only thought about in sci-fi books and movies.

JOHN CONNOR MEET BAXTER

We have moved one step closer to the intelligent machines foretold in the Terminator movies.

Baxter, produced by Rethink Robotics, represents a leap forward in industrial robots. Baxter's ability to work alongside humans makes it revolutionary for three reasons:

1. It can perceive humans around it and even show you where it is looking by shifting the "eyes" on its head. This allows Baxter to work around humans without injuring them.
2. It is trainable by anyone. You simply guide its arms through the correct motions and sequence of desired behaviors, and Baxter learns.
3. It is inexpensive, priced at $22,000.[3]

Granted, Baxter isn't going to take over complex jobs today. But, it is only a matter of time before many of Baxter's progeny and cousins will offer an alternative that is faster, better, cheaper, and, yes, friendlier.

CASE STUDY: IF THE GOVERNMENT GETS IT, WHY DOESN'T EVERYONE?

Money magazine ranked Carrollton, Texas, number 15 on its 2008 list of best small cities in which to live. This community of just over 120,000 in population occupies 37 square miles in northwest Dallas and southern Denton counties.

On the surface, Carrollton is similar to many communities throughout the United States. It provides quality public safety, streets, water, and sewer services. It has libraries, a senior center, and quality parks and recreation facilities and programs.

Dig deeper and you will find a commitment to doing everything faster, better, cheaper, and friendlier permeating every area of the operation. Staffing has decreased from 939 positions in 1995 to 843 positions in 2009 as the population has increased by more than 25 percent. City staff maintained service levels, and citizen satisfaction remains high. All of this was accomplished as the city's governing council held the tax rate steady, even during the economic challenges of 2009 to 2010.

In a profession where the business model is often an either/or decision to raise taxes or lower services, Carrollton has changed the game. Their effort is driven by three things:

1. A strategic goal to operate the city as a service business. This goal, set and sustained by its elected officials since 2001, serves as a constant expectation for urgency and continual improvement.
2. The successful creation of a managed competition process that requires departments to "earn their keep" every three years by showing that they are substantially competitive with the cost of the private sector to deliver the same type and level of service.
3. A commitment to transforming and sustaining the culture so that every person sees continual change as the great opportunity rather than the latest management buzzword or fad.

Leonard Martin, city manager, and Tom Guilfoy, director of competition, are the organizational face of the change. But the real story is an organization-wide culture where everyone gets it. Faster, better, cheaper, and friendlier are the standard by which every business is measured today.

So here is the question for you: What are your customers demanding for you to earn and retain their loyalty?

CHANGE LEADER ACTION LIST

1. Burn the boats. Your customers are in charge of defining expectations. You must send the message that maintaining or returning to the status quo is not an option.
2. Evaluate faster, better, cheaper, and friendlier through the best of your customers' experience. Find out the businesses that represent the best from your customers' perspective. Do everything you can to meet or exceed that level of performance. And remember, you are

(*continued*)

(*continued*)

being evaluated against that experience consciously or subconsciously all of the time.

3. Bring a sense of continuous curiosity and dissatisfaction to the discussion. Ask questions that force you to look beyond the status quo at every opportunity. The quality of the answers we receive are in direct proportion to the quality of the questions we ask.

Change is no longer an event. It is a way of life in constant pursuit of delivering results that are faster, better, cheaper, and friendlier.

Chapter 3

GOOD CHANGE,
BAD CHANGE

Change is neither good or bad. It simply is.

—Don Draper

TAKE THIS TEST

Everyone evaluates change through his or her own lens and experience. Here are eight changes common to everyone reading this book. Please take a moment to evaluate them.

		Good Change	Bad Change	Don't Know or Don't Care
1.	The rise of social media (Twitter, Facebook, Google+, LinkedIn, YouTube, etc.)			
2.	The expansion of mobile digital technology (smartphones, tablets, etc.)			
3.	The effect of European sovereign debt crisis on the global economy			
4.	The overthrow of governments and rise of democracy in the Arab Spring of 2012			
5.	The implementation of a new policy or process for the team on which you work (pick one)			
6.	The implementation of a new policy or process for a team in another department at the place where you work (pick one)			

(continued)

(*continued*)

		Good Change	Bad Change	Don't Know or Don't Care
7.	The passage of a new law in the country where you live (in the United States, let's go with the Affordable Care Act/ObamaCare)			
8.	A change in the location of your three favorite television channels on the cable or satellite network you use			

There are no inherently right or wrong responses to any of these changes. For instance, you could think the rise of social media is a good change because it provides a way to connect with friends and family, which increases the shared experience and connection.

Or social media could be a bad change because it is a detractor to meaningful, face-to-face conversation as everyone tweets and posts during dinner. And maybe you just don't care because you and your circle of friends don't participate in social media.

The same can be said of any change listed. Some people will think it is a good change; others, a bad change. And there are people who don't really know for sure or don't care.

THE COMMON FACTORS

There are seven common factors we all use to evaluate our response to change:

1. *How does it affect me?* A new policy in another department might be a good thing if it makes it easier for you to complete your work. It will be a bad change if it makes it harder. But chances are that you don't really care or have little more than a passing interest about the change if it doesn't affect you. The same can be said for big societal changes. The European sovereign debt crisis is a big deal if you live in Athens, Greece. It is probably not as important if you live in Athens, Texas. If it changes what you do or experience every day, it is a big change.

2. *How does the change move me/us toward something that I/we want or need?* Does it add value or move me/us toward a goal? Social media is an excellent tool for reconnecting with former class-mates from your high school. Whether that's something you need or want can be debated.

3. *Are the costs of changing less than the costs of staying the same?* Or put another way, is the pain of staying the same greater than the pain of changing? The decision to participate in the dem-onstrations of the Arab Spring cost many people their lives. For them, the cost of staying the same clearly outweighed the cost of trying to change things. There were, no doubt, others who supported the change, but active participation was not worth the cost.

4. *How much do you know about the change, and how much credibility does the person who is communicating it have with you?* One per-son's Affordable Care Act is another's ObamaCare. It is the same legislative change, but perception about the change is based on agreement with its goals and, to a large degree, the credibility of the person framing our perceptions about it. Many people (including elected officials on both sides of the argument) never read the details of the Affordable Care Act before forming an opinion about it.

5. *How much influence can I have on the change process?* You are more likely to feel that the process change on your team is a good one if you had an opportunity to influence the out-come. Likewise, it would be a great change if your television provider asked you to determine the location of channels on their network. You don't really care if you don't watch television.

6. *Did the change actually produce a result that is different and valu-able?* This observation from a seasoned manager early in my career still rings true today: "Just because things are differ-ent, that doesn't mean that anything has really changed." Chances are that you, like me, have seen changes that didn't produce results. That doesn't mean that you should never change anything unless you are sure of the final outcome. It does mean that you have to pay attention and fine-tune your work processes and habits to ensure results.

7. *How does this change add to or reduce my overall ability to func-tion and cope?* Moving your favorite television channel is less

stressful if you have ample time to leisurely browse for the new location. It moves from simply being a bad change to being a catastrophic one if the series finale of your all-time favorite show is starting in less than 1 minute and you have no idea where to find the new location, the battery is dead on your remote, and your family is yelling, "The show is starting! The show is starting!" in unison at the top of their lungs—not to mention that your spouse had asked you 20 minutes earlier if television was on the correct channel and you had given your assurance that everything was ready.

DEFINING A GOOD CHANGE

Results rule! It is as true today as it was in 2006 when I wrote the book by the same title. Using that criterion in its most literal meaning, any change that produces a desired result is a good change. Any collateral carnage associated with the change is simply the cost of doing business.

A few people suggested to me that a book titled *Results Rule!* epitomized everything that was wrong with the way business is conducted. Those people didn't read the book. If they had, they would have known that the only way to consistently deliver results is through sustaining a culture that builds and leverages partnerships based on trust.

It is the same with evaluating successful change efforts. You can wrestle any change into submission with enough brute force, time, and money. That will work once or maybe even twice. It is, however, a lousy way to run a business.

A good change, in my view, is one that achieves the desired result while causing no residual damage to relationships or excessive strain on resources. A good change is one where those involved feel as if they are engaged, involved, appreciated, and treated with respect for their contribution. A good change is as concerned with how the effort was completed as it is with the results of the effort.

Every change is evaluated against the seven criteria listed earlier in this chapter. Ignore those that affect the people side of the change (feelings and perceptions), and it is only a matter of time before the desired results suffer, too.

The type of change needed in today's successful organizations is continuous. It is generated from every level, and it requires engagement and commitment from those involved. You can mandate compliance. Commitment and engagement to make change work are volunteered when you focus on more than the end result.

WHY CHANGE FAILS

Think of a change in your organization that did not go as smoothly as you had hoped or achieved the result that you wanted.

Why? What were all of the things that could have been done differently or more effectively to have made that change work?

Here are the top 10 reasons I see, in no particular order. Take a few minutes to identify specific examples and the actions you would take in the future.

1. Planning or resource allocation is lacking.

   _____
   _____
   _____
   _____
   _____

2. The goal, purpose, or result is not defined. People don't know why the change is important or what it is supposed to achieve.

   _____
   _____
   _____
   _____
   _____

3. There are no measures or metrics in place to evaluate success.

   _____
   _____
   _____
   _____
   _____

4. There is no accountability. It doesn't matter if it works or it doesn't.

   _____
   _____
   _____
   _____
   _____

5. There is no buy-in for the change. Communication is lacking or even nonexistent.

_____

_____

_____

_____

6. There are no processes or guidelines to make sure that every-one knows what to do.

_____

_____

_____

_____

7. Leaders say that things are changing, but they never answer "from what to what?"

_____

_____

_____

_____

8. We allow resistance to derail the change.

_____

_____

_____

_____

9. Leaders move on to the next change or initiative before this one is completed or anchored in the organization's culture. We never give the change a chance to take hold.

_____

_____

_____

_____

10. We take on too many things at one time.

_____

_____

_____

_____

WHY CHANGE IS SO HARD

Change, by definition, causes at least some level of discomfort. If it happens easily and overnight, there is no real change.

Don't you hate that?

That is simply the way it works. There are six fundamental principles that make it difficult for people and organizations to be nimble and agile. Understand them, and you significantly increase the opportunities for good change to occur.

1. *The ability to change is based on readiness. Intellectual understanding is not the same as emotional readiness.* I spoke to groups as small as 5 or 6 and as large as 600 during my year as chairman of the American Heart Association for the state of Texas. I asked the same three questions at every opportunity:
   - How many of you know that you should eat healthier than you eat today?
   - How many of you know that you should exercise more than you exercise today?
   - If you smoke, how many of you know that you shouldn't do so?

   My guess is that you—like the majority of people in my audiences—were nodding your head or mentally raising your hand as you read those questions. We all know intellectually what we should do to improve our health—but that doesn't mean we are emotionally ready.

   It is the same way for people in organizations. They know that the need to work faster, better, cheaper, and friendlier. They simply aren't emotionally ready to do that every day.

2. *Past experience influences perception, and perception influences every aspect of the change process.* We all carry the baggage of previous experience. Some of us carry small overnight bags. Others of us haul large steamer trunks on our backs. Some of the bags are filled with bad experiences, and some contain good experiences. Either way, the change you want to make is being evaluated against past experiences. Those perceptions form a powerful point of view that influences receptivity and enthusiasm for change.

3. *Adapting to change is really about managing disrupted expectations. The larger the disruption, the more challenging the task.*

An unexpected crisis or disaster is the ultimate example of disrupted expectations. It is not uncommon to see people walking around in a semidazed state after a natural disaster. They are functional, but just barely. The enormity of disrupted expectations overcomes them. The same is true in organizations. An unexpected layoff, for instance, has a lingering effect that lasts for weeks or months.

This principle also affects how we handle small changes. Rolling out a new strategic plan may cause very little concern because it doesn't have an impact on your expectations. But changing where people park or when they go to lunch makes them crazy because it totally disrupts their expectations.

4. *Change always comes with a cost, even if the change was positive and you participated.* Have you ever been in a committed relationship with another person? At the time you entered it, did you think that was a positive change? Did it cost you something?

    This is the corollary to managing disrupted expectations. There is a cost to every change—even the positive ones. Ignore or underestimate the cost, and your change will take longer to implement and yield less-than-expected results.

5. *We live in a state of perpetual transition that prevents us from anchoring changes.* William Bridges wrote: "It isn't the changes that do you in, it's the transitions."[1] The idea is that every change has three parts:
    * An ending where the old way is over
    * A transition period during which there is a great deal of turmoil and discomfort
    * A new beginning where things are back to normal

    Kurt Lewin, the founder of Social Psychology, took a similar approach to change by saying that you unfreeze something that you want to change, make the change, and then refreeze the new behavior or thinking. The idea of starting an ending change still works at some level. For instance, there is an ending, transition period, and new beginning when you are implanting a new computer process.

    But more and more of the changes you are being asked to lead are continuous and never ending. Another change starts before the current one is complete. Even the changes with clear endings and new beginnings are experienced in the context of all the other changes that are competing for energy, attention, and resources.

We live in a perpetual state of transition. We no longer refreeze a new change. We simply put it in a Jell-O mold and hope it doesn't melt on the floor.

6. *Focusing on change* management *rather than change* leadership *places the focus on process not people.* Don't get me wrong. I love processes. Continuous improvement is a must to do things faster, better, cheaper, and friendlier. Clear processes are critical for refreezing new behaviors and performance. When it comes to change—especially the big, transformational type—no one wants to be managed into uncertain and unknown territory. People want to be led, and that means it will often feel messy and out of control. You can, with enough effort, take the uncertainty out of processes. That just doesn't happen with people.

CHANGE LEADER ACTION LIST

An important step for getting better at change is to stop shooting yourself in the foot by doing the wrong things. Think back on your change efforts and initiatives for the past two years and answer the following questions:

1. What are the examples of good change and bad change we have initiated and implemented? What lessons can we learn from those experiences?
2. Where have we failed to adequately consider the people side of change leadership and focused too heavily on the process side of change management?
3. Have we added to the feeling of perpetual transition for our people? Have we missed opportunities to minimize the impact of that reality?
4. What could we have done differently or better to create emotional readiness to change?

(*continued*)

(*continued*)

5. Are there situations where we did not accurately understand the cost of change in time, energy, and resources? What was the impact of that failure?

6. What are the lessons we can learn from the exercise about why change initiatives fail to achieve their desired results? What must we do to minimize those shortcomings in the future?

Chapter 4

DODOS AND COYOTES

Only the Nimble Survive

When we are no longer able to change a situation—we are challenged to change ourselves.

—Viktor E. Frankl

IN DEFENSE OF THE DODO

The dodo bird has become the iconic symbol for failure to adapt to a changing environment. The term *dodo* has come to be identified with a lack of common sense and being perpetually confused.

You could say that the dodo became complacent and comfortable. Dodos, however, were not born with the brain power to understand the concept of urgency, complacency, and change. The book *Jonathan Livingston Seagull*[1] taught the lessons of a young bird that strived to do more than fill his belly with scraps of food. But remember, that is a work of fiction.

Despite the modern connotations of being a dodo, the actual bird didn't have much of a choice. In fact, it never saw the danger coming. The entire species became extinct less than 100 years after its discovery and first interaction with humans.

The dodo bird was approximately 1 meter (3.3 feet) tall and weighed about 20 kilograms (44 pounds). Its native environment had no natural predators. As a result, it laid its eggs on the ground. And fatefully, rather than fleeing those first sailors who landed on its native island of Mauritius, the dodo approached them out of curiosity.

Imagine you were a sailor on that first ship landing on Mauritius. Would the sight of a bird that walks up to you while you're holding a club be an enticing thought? Don't you think you would be ready to try some fresh bird meat after months on a ship?

It is actually a miracle that the dodo lasted as long as it did. Direct human contact didn't hasten the dodo's extinction. It wasn't because humans valued the bird, however. Like many things, it was the secondary level of unintended consequences that did the dodo in.

The sailors found dodo meat to be tough and not particularly tasty. On the other hand, the cats, rats, pigs, and monkeys traveling with the humans loved the fact that dodo eggs were laid on the ground within easy reach. The feral dogs—not being as discriminating as the humans—no doubt found the dodo bird to be a fine meal.[2]

The dodo had a great life prior to the arrival of humans and predatory animals. It saw no reason to fly, much less to change, grow, and adapt. It had become genetically predisposed to being trustful of its environment. There was a time when it could have expanded the presence of the species by flying to other islands, but those days were long gone.

As a result, the dodo encountered by sailors in the 1600s was the victim of development in virtual isolation—no natural enemies, no need to extend its reach, and no time to adapt to a changing environment.

WHAT'S YOUR EXCUSE?

The dodos weren't stupid. They never had a chance. That's not the case with humans, and yet there are people, companies, and organizations of all shapes, sizes, and types who view their world through the eyes of the dodo bird.

Take a look at the factors that led to the dodo's demise and see if you find any similarities to organizations today:

- Grew up in a stable, secure environment with no need to worry about predators or outside danger
- Lost the ability to expand its reach out of comfort and complacency
- Had no ability to distinguish predators from friends
- Lost or never developed the ability to adapt quickly to changing opportunities or threats (primary and secondary)
- Never saw change coming or anticipated a different possible future and therefore left itself with no time to adapt

Dodos didn't know any better. You do.

IN PRAISE OF THE COYOTE

The Road Runner cartoons[3] featured Wile E. Coyote as the bumbling nemesis trying to capture the endlessly out of reach object of his desire. If you believe cartoons (and there are people who do), the coyote is not too far removed from the dodo bird in its ability adapt and survive.

The truth is far different.

The coyote may well be the model for nimbleness and adaptability in today's world. Granted, the coyote is not as sexy or mysterious as the legendary wolf. It isn't as cute as the mice or penguins that inhabit other popular change parables. And it is not as elegant as the dolphin and whale. But consider these facts:

- Coyotes originally inhabited open prairies and deserts in the southwestern part of North America. Today, they can be found from Alaska to Central America. They have expanded their habitat to forest, mountains, and urban areas.
- Whereas most species have found their existence threatened by the introduction of humans into their environment, coyotes have thrived in areas where humans live. They often do this without humans even knowing that they are there.

Coyotes are often the bane of farmers, ranchers, and owners of small pets. They will attack livestock, destroy gardens, and kill pets left unprotected. They may look mangy sometimes, but the coyote just gets it done. Here's why:[4]

- *Opportunistic problem solvers with the willingness to adapt:* Coyotes solved the problem of humans taking over their environment by expanding. They left the deserts and learned to thrive in the mountains, forests, and cities. They learned to scavenge for the food that humans threw away if hunting was no longer feasible. They learned that survival meant doing different things as well as doing things differently. Coyotes will eat basically anything: mammals, insects, fish, snakes, fruit, food, and plants. My guess is that coyotes never had to be sent to a training program to be told to adapt. They just looked for opportunities and did it.

- *Excellent vision and sense of smell:* Coyotes can detect food and danger up to a mile away. In other words, it is hard to surprise a coyote. And they know you are coming before you know that they are around.
- *Speedy:* Coyotes can run at a respectable 40 miles per hour. That is not puma-like speed, but it is fast enough for them to stay away from their predators and catch their prey.
- *Territorial sense of ownership:* Like their cousins the dog, coyotes mark and defend their territory. What is theirs is theirs, and you will have to fight them to take it.
- *Suspicious and secretive when it serves them:* Biologists estimate that there are between 1,000 and 2,000 coyotes in the Chicago metropolitan area.[5] Have you seen them strolling the neighborhood? Me either. Coyotes have developed the ability to hide in plain sight, and they will even walk on their toes to keep their prey from hearing them.
- *Strong family groups that take care of their young:* Coyotes mate for life. More important, their strong sense of family means that they increase their opportunities for protecting and growing the species. Male coyotes are active participants in caring for newborn pups, which means more of them survive.[6]
- *Versatile and willing to work alone, in teams, and even with other animals to succeed:* Coyotes usually work alone or in small packs of two or three. But they will expand to work in larger teams when it serves their purpose. Often, a larger pack of coyotes will include relatives of all ages. The old help the young and vice versa. Their versatility even extends outside of their species. Coyotes will often team up with badgers to track and kill a common prey. This isn't a matter of friendship. The coyotes and badgers want the same thing. They enter into this partnership of convenience because it conserves energy and increases their mutual effectiveness. Coyotes working with badgers in the desert catch an estimated one-third more ground squirrels than if the coyotes operate alone.[7]

CHANGE LEADER ACTION LIST

The future belongs to the coyotes. The dodos will become extinct.

So which one is your team or organization?

We have condensed the characteristics of these two animals into a 10-question assessment. This isn't scientific, but your responses will give you a glimpse of where you are and where you need to improve.

Here is the rating scale:

1. This is never how we operate.
2. This is how we operate and what we do occasionally or some of the time.
3. This is how we operate and what we do about half of the time.
4. This is how we operate and what we do most of the time.
5. This is how we operate and what we do all of the time.

		1	2	3	4	5
1.	We view our environment as constantly evolving and sometimes unpredictable—there is a keen sense of danger and/or opportunity.					✓
2.	We never allow a sense of comfort or complacency to prevent us from change.			✓		
3.	We move quickly and with a sense of urgency in pursuit of our goal once we decide to go.		✓			
4.	We have a strong sense of ownership. What is ours is ours, and others aren't going to take it.			✓		
5.	We readily collaborate—even with competitors—if it will help us succeed.	✓				
6.	We meet problems head-on with ideas to resolve them. We don't give up; we are resilient.		✓			

(continued)

(continued)

		1	2	3	4	5
7.	We are suspicious and secretive when it serves us; we don't hide from each other, but we know how to avoid or minimize predators that can harm us.					
8.	We know and can readily recognize our predators and our friends.			✓		
9.	We take care of our teams to ensure that they have everything they need to thrive and increase our mutual success.				✓	
10.	We are versatile and willing to try new things or develop new skills.					✓

Scoring

How close are you to becoming the nimble, adaptive, opportunistic problem solver that you need to be to make change work? This scale will give you an idea.

- 10–15: You are a first-class dodo. I wish there was another way of saying it, but your organization or team needs help now.
- 16–25: You are a dodo in the making. There is still time to turn it around, but it is going to take some work.
- 26–35: You aren't beyond hope, but you can't wait around forever to start changing.
- 36–44: You are well on your way to adopting the traits of the coyote. Your challenge is to keep learning and growing.
- 45–50: You are well positioned to make change work in today's complex and unpredictable environment. Congratulations!

Refer back to this scale often as you cover the next section about leading change. And remember, the characteristics that work for your organization will also work for your career. You need to be a coyote, not a dodo.

Part II

BECOMING
A CHANGE LEADER

The Tactical Side of Change

Chapter 5

WHAT CHANGE
LEADERS DO

Our dilemma is that we hate change and love it at the same time; what we really want is for things to remain the same but get better.

—Sydney J. Harris

THEY ARE DRIVING ME CRAZY!

Allan was at his wits' end. The transformation team he was leading was in chaos. Their work was stalled, and the carefully crafted timeline for completing their project was in danger of being obliterated by discord, disagreement, and, in a few cases, near-mutiny.

His frustration leapt from the screen as I read his e-mail requesting a call. During the conversation, Allan talked about how well everyone worked together as they created the change management charter, identified stakeholders, created their plans, and began their work. The plan was a good one. A few of the team members were simply allowing their personal discomfort with the change to get in the way of the work to be done.

HE'S DRIVING US CRAZY!

The team was in chaos. Allan—yes, that one—was driving them crazy. He refused to deviate from the change management plan. When a team member disagreed with the next action to be taken, he threw the timeline and project scope back on the screen and reminded everyone of the upcoming deadline. When someone raised a concern or allowed any doubt to drift into his or her work, he ignored it.

From the team's perspective, Allan was held captive by the project plan and wouldn't (or couldn't) allow any of the human element associated with the change to even be considered.

CHANGE MANAGEMENT AND CHANGE LEADERSHIP

I met with the team, including Allan, a few days later. The discussion was tense at first as everyone proudly announced their position and then worked to defend it. The atmosphere changed when we discussed the role of change management and the importance of change leadership.

As it turns out, everyone was right—and wrong. Allan was right that the project was in danger of missing important deadlines for which he was being held accountable. This was an important assignment with visibility to the highest levels of leadership. Missing deadlines could reflect poorly on his capabilities. Plus, he genuinely believed in the transformation at hand even though he wouldn't really be affected after its implementation.

The team was right, too. This project was important for them, but it was also deeply personal.

They and their coworkers back on the job would be asked to work in a dramatically changed structure and environment. Reporting relationships and work processes were going to change. Rumors were rampant that some could lose their jobs.

Allan was doing a masterful job on the task he was assigned. His change management plan covered all the steps and projected all the timelines. It outlined the deliverables and allocated the resources. It considered everything except one important piece— the feelings and emotions of the team.

The team wanted things to get better, but they were struggling with not wanting things to be different. They didn't need management as much as they were starved for leadership.

LEFT BRAIN AND RIGHT BRAIN

You have heard or seen the idea that different parts of the brain control different types of behavior, right?

People with left-brain dominance are often described as being good at logic, reasoning, and numbers. They are linear thinkers who start at step 1 and proceed in an orderly, efficient manner until the project is completed. It is not that the left-brainers don't have emotions. They do. They simply work to control them and not let them influence getting the job done.

Right-brain-dominant people are intuitive and creative. They are great at building relationships and are more tuned into feelings. Right-brainers can be good at numbers, logic, and reasoning, but their natural tendency is to favor intuition and feelings.

Change management, at least the way it is practiced by many, is primarily a left-brained activity. The focus is on charters and steps and timelines. Change is couched and managed in terms of projects, initiatives, or even projects within initiatives.

Allan, our team leader from the beginning of the chapter, adopted a left-brained linear approach to change management. He had clear starting and completion dates. Responsibilities were clearly defined, and he was proceeding in a very orderly fashion right up until the point that human emotion entered the equation. This level of detail and focus is helpful to keep things moving and ensure that all the project milestones and goals are met. What it doesn't do is help people feel connected, energized, and relevant.

Change leadership is a decidedly right-brained activity. It realizes that when it comes to people, the shortest distance between two points isn't necessarily a straight line. It is often a stroll or two around the block.

This type of leadership requires you to intuitively know when it is time to slow down and let your group catch its breath. Most important, it takes a big-picture view of the entire change and searches for connections to help everyone connect the dots about why it is important to the mission and vision.

Change management works if your goal is to define and complete a series of tasks in a project. Change leadership, however, is the best approach if the goals are to keep people connected, view their roles as relevant to the mission, and free them to be nimble rather than guarded in their responses.

WHAT CHANGE LEADERS DO

You didn't really think you could make it through an entire book without a change model did you? (See Figure 5.1.)

The right-brainers will immediately recognize the holistic nature of this model. The left-brainers are hoping that there is a logical sequence of steps for implementing it.

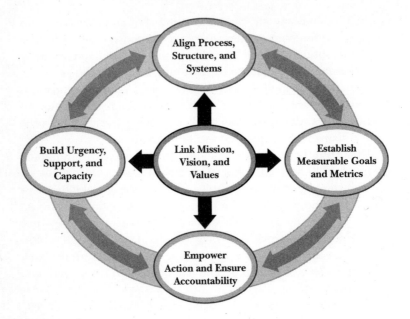

Figure 5.1   Change Leadership Model

Sorry, left-brainers. There is a clear starting point, but the sequence for everything else in the model is basically, "It depends."

The following seven steps are offered in a linear fashion and in as close to a logical order as possible to fit the confines of a book and make those looking for sequential steps a little less crazy. We'll expand on the strageties and techniques to succeed with the model in the chapters that follow, so please take this for what it is—a short description of what must be accomplished to successfully make change work.

1. *Link the change to the mission, vision, and/or values.* If the change you are considering doesn't advance your mission, move you toward your vision, or help you better live your values, why are you even considering it?

2. *Build the sense of urgency.* We devote an entire chapter to generating creative tension. In the meantime, suffice it to say that there are very few people who want to take on change for the sake of change. You will need to provide a compelling reason for the change to break the inertia that keeps most of us doing what we've always done.

3. *Establish measurable goals and metrics.* This step helps maintain urgency, and it defines what success looks like. It also helps the numbers people know that you aren't out chasing windmills in your mind. Most important, it sends a clear message about what is expected to be different as a result of this effort.

4. *Start building support.* You can't have too much communication about change. Well, maybe you can, but I have never seen it in more than 20 years. Building support begins with creating urgency, and it continues by helping others see why the change is important and enlisting their help. It is an ongoing process, and it is just about the time you start to tire of this effort that you are actually starting to make an impact.

5. *Align process, structure, and systems.* This is where the work gets done. We're using the word *alignment*, but recognize that this can also involve creation or reengineering. The leader must accomplish two goals at this point: (a) ensuring that the change does what it is supposed to do and (b) ensuring that the entire organization is aligned and capable of supporting and sustaining the change.

6. *Continue building support and start building capacity.* Knowing about something, or even knowing that you want to do something, is not the same as knowing how to do it. Make sure that everyone has the capacity (knowledge, skills, and resources) to successfully implement the change.

7. *Empower action and ensure accountability.* Give people control and allow them to try. They will make mistakes. That is what people do when they are trying something new and different. And ensure accountability. Now is the time to use the goals and measures to make sure that you are getting the results you want.

CAN YOU SKIP STEPS?

Even I fall into the trap of thinking of these in sequential order. Remember, these are items that you must accomplish to lead change. The amount of time, energy, and resources you invest in each will be based on the need and not on a prescribed set of activities. For instance, devoting a lot of time to building a sense of urgency is counterproductive if the company is about to collapse and everyone knows it.

Leadership is both a skill and an art. You can learn specific skills to become more effective. The art comes from knowing when to use the right skill. That is never truer than when you are leading change.

CHANGE LEADER ACTION LIST

Think back on two changes that you have implemented in the past. One should be your most successful change. The second should be one of your least successful changes.

Analyze what you did well and what you could have done better against the seven factors for leading successful change covered in this chapter.

Most Successful Change	
Where we did the best job with this change.	
Where we needed improvement with this change.	

Least Successful Change	
Where we did the best job with this change.	
Where we needed improvement with this change.	

Chapter 6

BUY-IN

Where Change Legends Are Made

Faced with the choice between changing one's mind and proving that there is no need to do so, almost everybody gets busy on the proof.
—John Kenneth Galbraith

THERE WAS DANCING AND SINGING

"We are BSC, and I've got all my people with me."

Can you hear the melody from the 1979 dance hit by Sister Sledge? The 200 or so employees of the newly developed Business Service Center (BSC) at the University of North Texas (UNT) System could, and they were having a great time.

The event was the official kickoff of a new organizational structure that had been in the active planning and development stages for nine months and talked about for at least a year before that.

Today was the official kickoff led by the newly created leadership team. It included speeches, Q&A sessions, a frank discussion of the vision and desired culture, and, most important, open dialogue about what the changes meant for the UNT System, the internal customers served by the BSC, and the employees themselves.

At the end of the 3-hour session, work teams had met for the first time with their new leadership and coworkers, and they caught a glimpse of the enthusiasm of their leaders.

A LONG TIME COMING

The outcome of this session would have been different nine months earlier. The campuses within the UNT System had traditionally operated as autonomous organizations at every level. The idea of traditionally back-office areas functioning in a shared services environment had been met with a range of emotions from open enthusiasm to open contempt.

Every attempt had been made to keep all stakeholders at all levels informed and engaged. Communication sessions were held.

Blogs were written. Questions were answered, and groundwork was laid. The kickoff session represented the end of the planning phase and the commencement of the implementation.

FAST-FORWARD ACROSS TOWN

Three months later, the UNT System IT Shared Services (ITSS) team met in a similar session. There was no dancing and singing this time. That would have been wildly inconsistent with leadership's personality. But there were the same opportunities for people to understand the details of a change that would, over time, dramatically alter how customers were served and employees were engaged.

Like its BSC cousin, this was the culmination of an organized and concerted effort to build understanding, acceptance, and support of the change. The leadership openly answered every question. When no answer was immediately available, they acknowledged it, captured the question, and communicated the process for addressing the issue or concern. Most important, the ITSS leadership sent these clear messages:

- The vision for the future and an open discussion of the gaps between current reality and the future state
- What specifically is changing and what areas are staying the same
- What the change means for the operation and the individuals, including the impact on what staff would be doing and how they would be working
- The results that were expected and how they were going to be measured
- Their confidence in the individuals on the team to make this change work
- Their personal support for the vision and the change
- Their awareness that everything would not be perfect from day 1 and that this event marked a transition point into the next phase of the change process

TWO STYLES—SIMILAR RESULT

Most, but not everyone, walked out of both of these kickoff sessions with a feeling of confidence and anticipation. The communication and engagement styles were different, but the same objectives were met.

Questions and challenges remained, but now there was a vehicle for addressing them. Those who were more skeptical by nature were still the most skeptical at the end of both sessions. But at that moment, these two change efforts had achieved that allusive place where legendary changes are made: buy-in.

WHAT IS BUY-IN?

For some, buy-in is demonstrated in that motivational moment of unity, like the singing and dancing of the BSC team. It is that point where everyone emotionally or physically locks arms and decides to slay the monster that is impeding the journey to greatness. For others, buy-in is the quiet confidence that recognizes the challenges ahead and their ability to overcome them.

Regardless of how it is demonstrated, buy-in is the point at which the people involved in the change—at least most of them—are actively working toward its success.

The absence of buy-in is reflected in any or all of the following ways:

- Benign apathy
- Open questioning
- Malicious obedience
- Sabotage (overt or covert)

WHEN BUY-IN OCCURS

Our experience shows that buy-in is most likely to occur when the following exist:

- There is a clear, compelling vision that describes the future—including what is expected to be different—and the good business reason to take on the change.
- There is a clear understanding that the cost of staying the same is outweighed by the risk of failing and/or the opportunity of succeeding.
- Individuals see what will be different for them and their teams and why that will be important for them.

- There is a belief and trust in the leadership to provide the resources, tools, and time to ensure success. The further the change pushes people out of their comfort zones, the more important it is that assurances be made that leaders will help others develop their capacities.
- Leaders demonstrate their personal buy-in, and there is a trust in their ability to lead the change.

NOT THE END

The job of getting buy-in with the BSC and ITSS organizations was over, right?

Hardly.

Most changes, including these, advance along a path that begins with high expectations, descends into a feeling of doubt or despair, and if the change is well executed, ends with the realization of success.

At every step of the way, the leader must reengage those on the change journey to stay the course.

MOSES, LINCOLN, KING, AND THATCHER

Moses found himself dealing with disgruntled Israelites during the journey to the Promised Land. Abraham Lincoln endured the pressure of bickering among his cabinet, ineffectiveness of his generals, and public response to the loss of life during the US Civil War.

Dr. Martin Luther King, Jr., wrote "Letter from Birmingham Jail" as both a response to the detractors of his cause and a motivation to his followers. And, in the face of opposition from Britain's traditional labor unions, Margaret Thatcher continued to make her case for the economic reforms in which she believed.

History is filled with leaders who challenged, supported, and engaged people to stay the course in moments when their vision and cause were in question. The job of building and sustaining buy-in for change is not a one-time activity. It is an ongoing effort that must continue until the change has become "just the way we do things around here."

MORE THAN A COMMUNICATION STRATEGY

The BSC at UNT System went from initial planning to implementation in less than one year. The ITSS operation did the same and introduced a unified IT governance process in less than nine months from inception.

The BSC saw a cost savings of approximately 13 percent in its first year of operation. The ITSS operation saw the growth of IT expenditures hold flat for the first time in recent history while keeping up with technology upgrades.

Support remains high . . . not perfect and not without challenges, but high. Almost two years into the change, the leaders continue to devote conscious attention to behaviors and actions that generate urgency and enhance support with stakeholders at all levels of the organization.

Most important, the leaders in both of these organizations are successfully changing the mind-set in their respective organizations from one that views change as a series of one-time events to one that embraces continual growth and change as just the way things are done in an effort to be faster, better, cheaper, and friendlier.

Their success has very little to do with a communication strategy designed to sell others on the need to change. The people they lead are like the people you lead—they have heard promises and seen new initiatives before. They are looking for real leadership, not the feeling of being sold something that they may or may not need.

CHANGE LEADER ACTION LIST

The chapters that follow will share six leadership strategies for creating urgency, building and maintaining support, and ensuring a successful change.

In the meantime, evaluate your last two or three change efforts.

1. Were you able to generate initial buy-in? If so, what did you do that helped you accomplish that? If not, what would you do differently in the future?
2. Were you able to maintain buy-in and support after the initial excitement subsided? What would you do differently, more of, or less of to maintain buy-in in the future?

Chapter 7

GO FIRST

Change is such hard work.

—Billy Crystal

CHANGE IS GOOD IF . . .

"Do things need to change around here?"

The answer to that question is always a resounding "Yes," followed by a list of changes others need to make. People in your organization are willing to change. They just want you to go first.

THE SURVEY SAYS . . .

How would you interpret this comment on an employee survey?

> All the Directors have posters with the promises and values. I see very little evidence that any of them have read or applied them in how they lead.

This was one of a very small minority of perceptions drawn from an employee survey about 20 months into a comprehensive organizational restructuring and culture change initiative. It isn't representative of the overall perception.

So why highlight it here?

The statement was made by a manager with immediate responsibility for implementing the new organizational structure and improving the culture in his area of the organization. Despite considerable work and organizational improvement, this manager chose to view the glass as half empty rather than half full. Rather than focus on what he needed to do—and there were a number of things that needed improvement—he chose to blame others.

There are always a few, aren't there?

CREATING REALISTIC OPTIMISTS

People react to change in one of four ways (see Figure 7.1):

1. *Unrealistic pessimists:* These individuals never give change a chance. You can show them an endless list of good reasons why the change is necessary and how it will work, but they will still be against it.
2. *Realistic pessimists:* These individuals see themselves as realists, and most of the time they are. They look at the facts and decide that the change won't work or should not be attempted. Realistic pessimists who point out legitimate reasons why a change can't work are valuable assets. Those who refuse to even consider how a change can be accomplished are liabilities.
3. *Unrealistic optimists:* These individuals never met a change that they didn't like. They embrace change for the sake of change and ignore the difficulties involved. Their enthusiasm is contagious. But like recovering from a virus that has runs its course, others eventually recover from their unrealistic displays of support.
4. *Realistic optimists:* These individuals acknowledge the challenges and choose to look for the opportunities to make the change work.

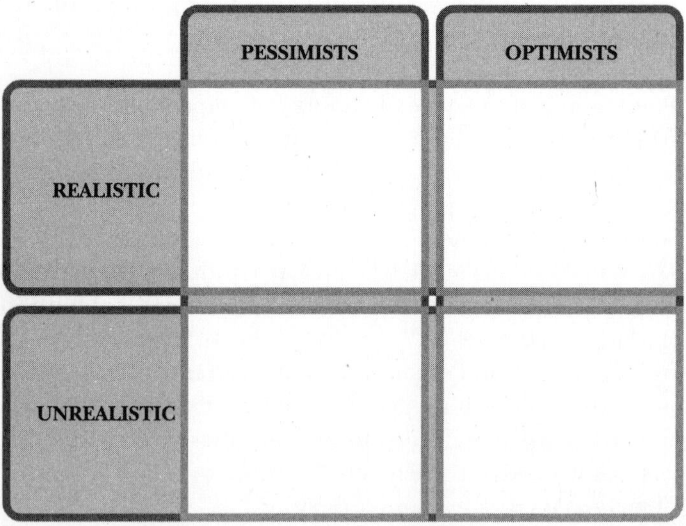

	PESSIMISTS	OPTIMISTS
REALISTIC		
UNREALISTIC		

Figure 7.1   Reactions to Change

PEOPLE CAN CHANGE WHERE THEY ARE

People are not automatically locked into one specific quadrant with their response. They can move from one to another based on the information they receive, their experience with the change, and most important, their willingness to avoid the three-dimensional (3D) vision that prevents them from seeing the truth.

3D vision is an affliction that prevents us from seeing the need to change and truth about change. It stands for

- Denial
- Distortion
- Delusion

We deny the facts, distort reality, and delude ourselves into unrealistic perceptions (positive or negative) about the need to change and progress toward its successful completion.

WHERE YOU COME IN

Change, to be effective and lasting, must be supported by enough realistic optimists to create a tipping point of support and commitment. Amassing this group of supporters is virtually impossible unless those in positions of influence demonstrate and model behaviors and attitudes that foster commitment and success.

Remember, compliance can be mandated; commitment is volunteered. Leaders must go first to build realistic optimists.

ARE YOU THERE YET?

Leaders who go first model the following seven behaviors. Take a few moments to rate yourself (or the leaders in your organization) on a 1 to 5 scale, with 5 being highest, to see how well you are doing.

		1	2	3	4	5
1.	Embrace change as an opportunity to move toward the mission, vision, and values.					
2.	Tolerate ambiguity as long as there are signs of progress.					

(*continued*)

(continued)

		1	2	3	4	5
3.	Avoid 3D vision—tell themselves and others the truth.					
4.	Create opportunities for others to own the change.					
5.	Value and recognize the level of work, energy, and resources required to make change work.					
6.	Are open to new ideas brought to them. Consider ideas based on their merit.					
7.	Recognize that everyone deals differently with change and tailor their approach for communicating and building support.					

HOW DID YOU DO?

This is not a scientific assessment. It is a safe assumption, how-ever, that the validity of your answers is in direct proportion to the honesty of your response. If you scored mostly 4s and 5s, you are modeling the types of behavior that create realistic optimism for change. If you scored 3 or less, you have work to do. Highlight those areas where you need improvement and pay special attention to the techniques covered here to help you get better.

HOW YOU KNOW YOU AREN'T THERE YET

There are two additional ways you can determine whether you are setting the example of going first:

1. Ask your team to complete the previous assessment to deter-mine how you are doing from their perspective.
2. Watch for the continued or consistent examples of any of the following behaviors:
   - Blaming others or circumstances beyond their control for the success or failure of the change
   - Assuming others are responsible for the success or failure of the change
   - Evaluating success by focusing on effort rather than results
   - Mandating compliance rather than getting volunteered commitment

CHANGE LEADER ACTION LIST

Your position earns you compliance. Your ability to influence earns you commitment. And there is nothing that enhances influence more than personal performance that is consistent with the words we say.

The action list for this chapter is simple:

1. Determine whether you are going first to set the example for change.
2. If not, identify areas where improvement is needed.
3. Look for strategies and techniques to help you improve in the chapters that follow.

Billy Crystal was correct. Change is hard work. But it is easier work for your team when they see that you are leading by example and not by decree.

Chapter 8

CHANGE CHANGE

Change before you have to.

—Jack Welch

WE CHANGE WHEN. . .

You change a lightbulb when it burns out. You change buses, trains, and airplanes when the one you're on won't take you to your desired destination. Athletic teams change head coaches and players when the team isn't winning.

Organizations change when . . . ?

If you immediately thought, "when things are broken or not going as well as we want," congratulations. Your view of change is like that of most people—when things aren't working.

WISE WORDS

When I got married, my wife said to me, "Randy, I'll never ask you to change."

I thought, "Cool."

She then went on to say, "I do, however, expect that you will continually adapt."[1]

It turns out that my wife had the perfect advice for succeeding in today's world. When you cease to adapt, you cease to remain relevant. And when you cease to remain relevant, you run the risk of becoming obsolete. And sooner or later, things that are obsolete are tossed aside—figuratively if not literally.

THE BIG "BUT"

Adapting quickly to change in the environment is essential to staying nimble and relevant. In fact, the most nimble organizations react so quickly that they almost appear to be ahead of the change.

Conversely, viewing change as reactive places you and your team in the position of always catching up with your competitors, customers, and industry. Over time, that type of change creates fatigue and causes burnout.

The most nimble leaders and teams see around corners and anticipate the needs of customers and opportunities within the marketplace before others. They remain hypervigilant regardless of the current level of performance or economic environment.[2] They take my wife's wise words literally and change before they have to.

ANOTHER CHANGE CLICHÉ

Clichés, at least before businesspeople overuse them to the point where no one stops to think about their true meaning, are based on truth. And when it comes to changing the way we think about change, there is no truer statement than this one by ice hockey great Wayne Gretzky:

I skate to where the puck is going to be, not where it has been.

The problem with this particular cliché is that it can be difficult to know where the puck is going to be. How much time do you have to study industry trends or think strategically about the future?

Most supervisors, managers, and leaders with whom I work feel lucky to carve out time for the occasional strategic planning or goal setting retreat. They try to keep up with ideas in in the business news and their professional journal. But judging from the stacks of month's old magazines piled behind their desks, many struggle to keep up with the new ideas that are shaping their industries and careers. Thinking about where the puck is going to be is a luxury they don't believe they have.

THE TIME TEST

Pull out your calendar. I can hear the groans as I am writing, but do it anyway.

This isn't going to turn into a time management seminar, but the reality is that your calendar is the true test of what is important to you. How much time did you invest over the past month thinking about the future and where your company, industry, or profession is going?

Don't feel bad if the amount of time is small or nonexistent. Mark Ellwood, president of Pace Productivity Inc., reported that only 2 percent of managers in his studies report any time spent on long-range planning that affects the future.[3]

Thinking about the future doesn't require a great deal of time. In fact, Ellwood found that the managers who did track their time in long-range planning wished that they could spend less time in that area.

But you do need to have some idea where the puck is going. How are you going to change your team's perception of change if you can't anticipate it for yourself?

Assuming you said that this is an area on which you need to focus, your goal is to make a small incremental improvement. If you are starting at zero, set a target of 15 minutes per week if you are a frontline leader. Keep working until you can get to 30 minutes per week.

Target 5 to 10 percent of your time for actively thinking about the future if you are a mid-level leader. The best senior leaders with whom I have worked devote 30 to 40 percent of their time on future related activities.

THE LENS IS AS IMPORTANT AS THE TIME

The present should be guided more by the future than the past. Unfortunately, most of us look at the present and even the future through the lens of what has worked in the past.

Remember, the goal is to alter the way you and your team think about change. If you are guided by the past, you tend to view change as, at best, a nuisance. If you are guided by the future, change is an opportunity to continually grow and adapt.

AFP AND MBBS

How do the people in your organization or team view and talk about change? Is it a pain, another program of the month . . . or worse?

I had the pleasure of following Richard Teerlink, former chief executive officer of Harley Davidson, as a speaker. His description of how employees described change when he began with the company generated a huge laugh: AFP . . . which is loosely and publicly defined as *Another Fine Program.*

One of my clients coined an equally colorful term to describe change at the large utility company where she worked as director of communication. She explained that her company had implemented a never-ending series of "management by_____" initiatives over the years. Now they all just called any change MBBS . . . which is loosely and publicly defined as *Management By Best Seller.*

CHANGE LEADER ACTION LIST

What would be different in your team or organization if every person at every level viewed change as an opportunity to get better rather than an assumption that something is broken or that management has been to another seminar?

You can begin to change the perception of change by consistently taking these four actions:

1. Change the Conversation and Language

Stop calling it change. Sounds easy, huh? It isn't. The word *change*, along with its negative connotations, exists everywhere. I'm not telling you to erase the word *change* from your vocabulary. That would be impossible and dumb.

Look for every opportunity to substitute *change* used in a negative connotation with other words that reinforce the positive aspects of adapting to stay relevant. Some of my clients use the language of continuous improvement. Others talk about living in a state of perpetual transition. A few others simply talk about adapting.

And they talk about it all of the time. They devote time in staff meetings to involving everyone in discussions about how to make things better or new trends. They expect that people attending conferences present the ideas they learned upon returning. They create time for people to share ideas about what works and ways to make things better. For example, one

IT client provides lunch one time per quarter for developers to share the shortcuts and new ideas they have developed for writing code.

Simply using a different word for change won't magically make it more pleasant to do things differently. It will, over time, reinforce that change is something that we do every day to get better and not only when things are broken.

2. Reinforce New Ideas That Promote Change

What gets reinforced gets repeated. So what are you reinforcing when it comes to new ideas that promote change? Are new ideas welcomed and applauded, or are they pushed aside with, "We've never done it that way before," or "I'll take that under advisement"?

Try this exercise: Ask your team to list all the "idea killer" phrases that they have heard in their careers. You can do this alone or among a group of peers if you want, but new ideas are killed from every level, not just by managers.

Groups with which I have done this activity can usually come up with a list of 50 to 100 phrases and words in less than 15 minutes.

Then list the words and phrases that promote and reinforce new ideas and change. You can generate a similar number of responses, but experience shows that they don't come easily or as quick.

The most important part of this exercise is to make a conscious effort to reinforce new ideas and language that promote change as a positive opportunity.

3. Change the Consequences

A later chapter is devoted to overcoming resistance. For now, let's focus on positive consequences. Who gets promoted? Who gets the merit increases? Who gets the opportunities to work on the cool new ideas?

It may become necessary to deal with those who do not change their view of change in a corrective manner. But

(continued)

(*continued*)

that isn't the best initial approach if you want to be a change leader rather than a change manager.

Most people want to do a good job. They want to help the team get better—and they will if given the opportunity and ability.

4. Work on Your Own Time and Perceptions

The time test you were asked to do earlier in this chapter is important. Most of the transformational changes we experience could have been anticipated if we knew where to look and had taken the time to do so.

■ ■ ■

The leaders, organizations, and teams who make change work don't view change as a negative. They embrace it as an opportunity to prove their continued relevance and responsiveness in a competitive marketplace.

Chapter 9

GENERATE CREATIVE
TENSION

People do things for their reasons, not yours.

—Unknown

A UNIVERSAL PRINCIPLE

Personal motivators and preferences for taking action have been a constant theme basically forever. The list of authors, speakers, and business consultants who have used the quote that opens this chapter is so extensive that it was impossible to determine who was the first.

So with nods to the legendary Zig Ziglar and several of my colleagues who have used this statement over the years, here is the truth as it relates to change:

> *People see no reason to help you make change work unless you give them one that is important to them.*

WHY WE CHANGE

The motivation and decision to change are based on emotional readiness. Intellectual understanding is not the same as emotional readiness.

This is a truth that makes change difficult—remember the discussion in Chapter 3—and it is a truth that makes change possible. People and organizations change for two basic reasons:

1. Crisis pushes them to change.
2. Opportunity pulls them to change.

Most people and organizations wait on crisis. You see that tendency in the heart attack survivor who becomes a zealot for good health after a near death experience. And, you see it in the companies who become zealots for good business practices after brushes with failure.

BURNING PLATFORMS AND POLITICIANS

Daryl Conner introduced the metaphor of the *burning platform* to create urgency for change in his book *Managing at the Speed of Change*.[1] Conner describes the explosion of an oil-drilling platform in the North Sea off the coast of Scotland in July 1998.

A total of 165 crew members and 2 rescuers lost their lives that night in July. Sixty-three crew members survived because they saw the crisis and jumped from the burning platform into the ice-cold waters of the North Sea.

Fast-forward to the year 2008. The United States is facing its own burning platform in the form of financial implosion. Rahm Emanuel had recently been appointed chief of staff for then-president-elect Barack Obama, and he made this statement at a *Wall Street Journal* forum:

> *You never want a serious crisis to go to waste. And what I mean by that is an opportunity to do things you think you could not do before.*

Emanuel's quote was vilified by his political opponents, but he was not the first and will not be the last to seize the opportunity to create a burning platform.

CRISIS CREATES URGENCY

During my college years, I worked for a company that manufactured diamond drill bits for oil drilling. Although I worked in shipping and in the shop, I was able to visit a few onshore drilling sites. And even though I never had the chance to visit an offshore rig, I always enjoyed talking to the sales guys when they returned to the plant and they would share what it was like to be on a rig out in the ocean.

The drilling rigs are about 150 feet from the platform to the water. There are things in the water that will hurt you. Depending on the part of the world you are in, there are even creatures in the water that will eat you. If you jumped into the North Sea that night of the explosion in 1998, you would have been doing so in darkness, with no idea where you would land.

The survivors who jumped from the burning platform into the North Sea didn't want to do so. This wasn't a recreational swim with the oil workers jumping and yelling, "Cannonball!" or their version of walking over hot coals at a personal development seminar.

Put yourself in that position. Would you jump?

Most of the people to whom I have asked that question respond, "Yes." And then they add that they would wait until the last minute to do so. In today's environment, the decision to wait can place you in a position from which you can never recover.

Crisis generates the tension between a desired future and impending reality that causes people to take action. In the face of crisis, people will do things that they had never considered possible or even plausible.

That is what Emanuel and every other politician knows. Leaders in organizations know it, too.

WE NEED TO SELL AGAIN

I was a partner in a small boutique consulting firm in a previous life. We were very successful most of the time, but about every two years we would hit a financial crisis. Sometimes the crisis resulted from the complacency that comes from believing you have made it. Other times, crisis arose from the reality that we had become so busy delivering our service that we didn't have time for business development.

Either way, the result was the same. We would realize that we had lost our focus on marketing and selling. Next we would run the numbers and realize that things needed to change. This would be followed by a renewed focus on business development and tough decisions to make difficult cuts to our expenses.

The final steps in this cycle of crisis were predictable:

- Everyone made changes to refocus energy on generating revenue and holding down costs.
- We would work our way out of the crisis and restore our profitability.
- We would slowly become happy and dumb until the cycle began again.

PEOPLE DO THE SAME THING

Between 50 and 80 percent of heart attack survivors return to previous unhealthy lifestyle patterns, according to Dr. Diana Hughes.[2] The reason is that the sense of urgency felt at the time of the crisis dissipates. They lose the tension that creates the urgency.

Seeing this take place over a number of years in individuals and organizations has taught me that lasting change based on the immediacy of a crisis is difficult to maintain.

CRISIS ABUSE

Yet there are leaders who continue to generate crisis after crisis after crisis as their tool of choice for generating urgency. If everything is a crisis, then eventually, nothing becomes a crisis. Don't waste a good crisis, but don't generate a bogus one. And certainly don't continually manufacture a series of fake crises. Doing so will cost you your credibility. Like Aesop's fable of "The Boy Who Cried Wolf," sooner or later people will stop responding.

OPPORTUNITY PULLS

Apple revolutionized the smartphone market with the iPhone. It created a new category of personal computing devices with the iPad. The change associated with these innovations was born out of opportunity not crisis.

The opportunity to do something important and meaningful can be a great motivator for change *if* leaders set the stage in a way that generates creative tension.

SHOW ME THE COOKIE

Imagine that you are the parent of a three-year-old. Your child walks into the kitchen and sees the ultimate prize on top of your refrigerator: a jar of Double Stuf Oreo cookies.

You know what is going through your child's mind, don't you? He or she is consumed with bridging the gap between the compelling vision of the cookies and the reality that he or she can't reach the top of the refrigerator.

And what will a child do to bridge that gap?

The short answer is everything. You don't have to say, "Be creative. Explore new opportunities. Think outside the box." All it takes is the opportunity presented by the cookies.

HOW ABOUT BRUSSELS SPROUTS?

Do you worry about your three-year-old inventing new ways to reach the top of your refrigerator if the cookies are replaced by brussels sprouts?

I didn't think so.

So here's the question: What is on top of your company or team's refrigerator? Are you trying to motivate others with Double Stuf Oreos or brussels sprouts?

WHAT BANKRUPTCY TAUGHT GENERAL MOTORS ABOUT URGENCY

Ed Whitacre, Jr., was named chairman of the board for General Motors (GM) after the company announced its bankruptcy in June 2009. One of his first acts was to meet with newly appointed chief executive officer, Fritz Henderson.

Whitacre says, "I had strong views as to what Fritz needed to do. To get GM back on track and employees reengaged, he was going to have to communicate a clear and compelling vision."[3]

The GM board of directors gave Henderson 90 days to show that he was up to the task of leading GM back to solvency and relevancy. His personal sense of urgency was, in Whitacre's mind, unquestioned. In addition, Henderson was a walking encyclopedia of facts and figures. The problem was that GM wasn't organized and run in a manner that capitalized on the very real crisis and showed the opportunity that could be achieved in the future. At the end of the 90-day probation period, Henderson was removed.

There is no doubt that Henderson could explain all the intellectual reasons why change was needed at GM. But he didn't do the right things to create the tension that leads to urgency and results in nimble execution.

CREATIVE TENSION

Change agents have a unique ability to put a crisis into perspective while creating a sense of hope about the future. They are truthful about where they are, honest about what it will take to make the necessary changes, and optimistic about the future.

They show people the cookies while acknowledging that bridging the gap between reality and vision is fraught with challenge.

It is a fine line to walk. If you sugarcoat the reality, people don't understand why there is an urgent need to change. If you can't show people hope for the future, they give up. If you define success only as survival, they are more likely to return to their old habits once the crisis has subsided.

Think of it as a guitar string. When tuned too tightly, it breaks under the stress. When tuned too loosely, it adds no value to the instrument. But when tuned with just the right amount of tension, it makes great music in the hands of a masterful guitarist.

The art of generating creative tension comes when you are so in touch with your team that you know when to focus on the crisis and when to create the vision of the cookies.

CHANGE LEADER ACTION LIST

1. Analyze what is on top of your refrigerator. Are you showing your team Double Stuf Oreos or brussels sprouts? If it isn't cookies, work on the compelling vision. Ask yourself this question: What could we achieve that would make doing this work so cool and so much fun that people couldn't wait to help us succeed?
2. When faced with a crisis that requires change, make sure that you do the following:
   - Tell people the truth. Don't sugarcoat the situation.
   - Provide hope and show your confidence. Your team needs to see that you have a vision for success.

- Let people know that you need them. Others have to see themselves as playing an important role in the effort.
- Recognize effort and give people feedback. Over-communicate during the crisis.

3. If you find yourself wanting to manufacture a crisis to generate urgency, don't. You either aren't working hard enough to find the legitimate crisis, or you aren't working hard enough to create a compelling opportunity. Either way, you will destroy your long-term credibility.

Chapter 10

CONNECT WITH PEOPLE WHERE THEY ARE

Change does not roll in on the wheels of inevitability, but comes through continuous struggle.

—Martin Luther King, Jr.

IMAGINE THIS

An e-mail arrives from the chief executive officer of your company with the following message:

> It is no secret that the past few years have been a struggle. Our competitors are buying market share at the expense of profitability. We must now undertake radical change to ensure our survival.
>
> As a result, we are embarking on a complete reorganization of your division. This change will allow us to streamline decision making, improve communication, increase efficiency, and focus all of our energy on customer needs.
>
> We are a great company with an outstanding team, and I know that we can be even better. We have a history of leading our industry. I know that with your support and commitment, we can regain that position.

What's on Your Mind?

The intended message was one of crisis and opportunity to generate the creative tension we discussed in the last chapter. Is that what was going through your mind?

Or were you worried about one or more of the following:

- How will we accomplish this reorganization and still complete the work?
- How is this going to affect our customers? Will it really be easier, or will we lose customers in the transition?

- Will this work? Do we have the capacity and capability to pull this off?
- What will happen to my teammates? How are they going to be affected?
- What will happen to me? Will I have to work longer hours? How will it affect my job?

Don't feel bad if you were not immediately engaged and energized by the corporate message. Scott Keller and Carolyn Aiken, consultants at McKinsey & Company, suggest that 80 percent of what leaders care about and talk about when trying to enlist support for change does not matter to 80 percent of the workforce.[1]

To gain the commitment for the change that you want, you must connect with people where they are.

COMPARISON SHOPPING

My father had a problem. He was the shop manager for the International Harvester tractor and truck dealership in the small town where I grew up, and his staff was upset about their pay.

Although there is no way human resources would ever allow his solution today, it was a novel approach at the time: My father asked each person in the shop to write down the salary he believed was deserved on a piece of paper and sign it. He reviewed all of the requests, judged them to be reasonable, took them to the dealership owner, and convinced him that each person should be paid the salary for which they had asked.

The members of his team were ecstatic . . . for a week.

The next Friday the shop was in chaos as some members of the crew discovered—after comparing their pay stubs—that they were paid less than others they judged as being equal in talent, effort, and productivity.

My father patiently pulled each person's piece of paper and asked if they had received the salary they said they deserved. Each reluctantly agreed that they had been given exactly that amount. My father told them that he had kept his end of the bargain and that he expected them to do the same. He also agreed to revisit the situation in six months.

We Compare Everything

The point of the story isn't compensation. It is the fact that we all compare. We do it with our worth, our favorite restaurants, and our favorite songs.

For more than 20 years, Dan Ariely has studied why people view and do things as they do. He has discovered that "people rarely choose things in absolute terms." In fact, we are often predictably irrational in how we determine our actions and our view of the world.[2]

This same irrational tendency to compare affects how we view and support change, too.

Your response to the e-mail exercise that opened this chapter was based on a comparison of your experience with other similar change efforts. For some, the response was compared with the experience and perception of others—even if it was totally irrational.

Unload the Baggage

I often ask participants in my presentations and workshops if any of them have moved into a new home over the past two years. There is always at least one.

My next question is: How long did it take you to become truly comfortable in your new environment? Responses range from six months to still not being completely settled into their new environment after two years.

The Exception

I asked the same question to one of the MBA groups with which I work at Southern Methodist University. I was caught off guard by one of the responses:

"Two weeks," the first-year student said.

"Really? Only two weeks?" I replied.

"Look," he responded. "It doesn't really take that long when all you have is an inflatable bed and a duffle bag."

We All Bring a Past

As we discussed in Chapter 3, each of us brings baggage to every situation.

Some of our bags are filled with good experiences, and some of it is filled with bad experiences. Some of it is rational. Much of it isn't.

Effective leaders help others understand and unload the negative stuff in their baggage to connect and engage them to actively participate in the change.

Okay, How?

Here is an effective tool that I have used in hundreds of change initiatives on which I have consulted and led. Ask everyone on the team to list all the reasons change efforts fail to reach their desired goal. You could rephrase the question to ask about what makes a successful change, but that list is usually much shorter. Remember, most change initiatives fail and all have challenges.

Allow people to share their examples for as long as the responses are flowing. There will be similarities, but do not point them out.

Every response represents one more piece of baggage that is being taken out and viewed. When all of the responses have ended, thank everyone for helping the team identify all the things that must be avoided if this change is going to deliver on the expected results.

Remember that everyone brings baggage that is often influenced by irrational perception. Some people will hold on to their baggage for decades. The process of unloading and acknowledging it helps you connect.

MAKE IT REAL AND RELEVANT

Recall from way back in Chapter 1:

- The biggest threat most of us face is relevancy. People who purchase your product or service are asking, "Why you? Why now? What makes you relevant?"
- Employers who are deciding to hire you or even keep you on the payroll are asking the same questions.

Let's extend further: The team you need to engage to make your change successful is asking those same questions, too. Based on the statistics from Keller and Aiken in their work at McKinsey & Company, most leaders do a lousy job at answering them.

WHAT WE SAY AND WHAT THEY HEAR

Joe Malarkey[3] has thrilled audiences around the globe with his unique perspective on success and motivation. Joe (operating through the highly creative and slightly warped comedic brain of veteran funny man George Campbell) has the unique ability to interpret corporate-speak through the ears of those on the listening end of a leader's communication.

I asked Joe to share what at least a few people are thinking when we fall prey to buzzwords and business generalities:

Your Message	Corporate-Speak Interpretation
This change will maximize our resources and align our efforts.	Stop stealing the paper clips.
This new process represents a sea of change for our business and industry.	Raise your hand if you know how to swim.
We plan to utilize the synergy between our business units to capture increased market share.	We accidentally bought our biggest customer.
We want to break through the clutter to create clarity around our messaging.	Shut up so I can talk.
This new change will create organic growth and ensure long-term sustainability.	We have this conference room booked through next Thursday.

WHAT THEY WANT TO HEAR

Granted, your team may interpret these phrases differently than Joe. But you can rest assured that they are processing them through the lens of their own experiences, concerns, perceptions, and values.

You connect to people when you make the change relevant and real. Here are the top five questions I hear from frontline employees as we talk about impending change:

1. *From what to what?* Tell me the specifics of what we will be different in how we must think, act, and perform.
2. *What does this change mean for what I do and how I operate on a daily basis?* This is the personal application extension of the previous question.

3. *Will this make a difference?* Is there a good business reason for doing this? How will it help the business or team? It is okay if the change is purely for compliance reasons. Just tell me.

4. *How will success be measured?* If you can't measure success, how will you know that there has been a return on our effort and investment? And how will you know whether to reward or hold me accountable for my participation?

5. *What is the support level for this change?* Do you, my boss, really believe in this, or is it another mandate from on high?

IT HELPS IF THEY BELIEVE YOU

Trust is the lubricant that removes friction from relationships. It gives people confidence to embrace change, and it empowers people to say what needs to be said without fear of reprisal.

Trust strengthens connection because I am sure of your motives. Trust allows me to hear difficult messages without misreading your intent.

PLANT THE GARDEN

My father planted tomatoes every year that I can remember. When I was young, he planted them in a flower bed along the side of our house. When I moved away, he created a small garden at about third base in our makeshift backyard ball field.

During all of those years, I never heard him say: "I just planted tomatoes out back. I hope we don't get cucumbers coming up." The law of the garden says, what you plant, when you plant it, and the care that you give it determine what your garden produces.

Earning trust—like growing tomatoes—doesn't occur overnight. The leaders who inspire credibility during change began planting that trust early in the relationship. They nurture it through the:

- Quality of their character
- Scope of their competence
- Consistency of their actions
- Clarity and timeliness of their communication
- Courage of their convictions

Once planted, trust enables you to connect in ways that strengthens buy-in and provides the benefit of the doubt when others feel the uncertainty of change.

CHANGE LEADER ACTION LIST

1. Before you begin your next change effort, invest the time to understand the baggage that stakeholders are bringing to the effort. Doing so will help you address their fears and concerns.
2. Remove—or at least minimize—the buzzwords and jargon from your communication. Make your message real and relevant to the listener. Remember, 80 percent of what you are inclined to say about change will not appeal to 80 percent of your audience.
3. Start now to plant the garden of trust and credibility. If you have that relationship, invest time to care for it. You will be glad you did when it comes time to deliver a difficult message about change.

Chapter 11

INVOLVE EARLY
AND OFTEN

Things alter for the worse spontaneously, if they be not altered for the better designedly.

—Francis Bacon

YOU CAN COUNT ON THIS

When it comes to successful change of any size or type:

- People support what they help create.
- People never argue with their own information and ideas.

The person who brings you the idea about a new work process will enthusiastically ensure its success. There is a good chance that the same change—recommended by you—will be met with reasons why it won't work.

This isn't new, and it isn't complicated. Most important, we know that it increases the opportunities for successful change.

Research conducted by the IBM Global Business Services Strategy & Change Practice found that the challenge of employee involvement ranked second (behind senior management sponsorship) out of the top 10 factors that contributed to successful change.[1]

WHY INVOLVEMENT DOESN'T OCCUR

Attitudes about employee involvement have evolved over the past 20-plus years. There was a time when leaders routinely adopted the my-way-or-the-highway approach to implementing a new process, procedure, or organizational structure. These days, the reluctance to involve others is focused more on *how* rather than *if* the involvement occurs.

You have five options:

1. *Awareness:* Provide the information others need about the change and how it will be implemented.
2. *Input:* Ask for feedback about the change and/or your plans to implement it.
3. *Participation:* Involve others early to understand their questions, concerns, and issues about the change. Ask for ideas about the desired result and their approach for getting there.
4. *Collaboration:* Work in partnership to develop a solution that meets everyone's needs.
5. *Empowerment:* Give others control over the decision and implementation. This could include asking for recommendations and then approving them.

There Is a Place for All Five

Buy-in for change is highest when all five levels are used at the right time and place. Here is how the leaders from the two shared services organizations discussed in Chapter 6 involved others:

- Awareness was an important tool to let everyone know what was happening in the change process, deal with rumors, and keep people informed regarding progress. This was done through e-mails, blog posts, and routine Q&A sessions.
- Input from key stakeholders was gathered at critical points during the planning and implementation using formal and informal strategies. The input gathered was used to gauge reaction to the direction the change was taking rather than to generate ideas.
- Participation occurred initially at the leadership levels as the initial plans for merging similar functions from separate entities were completed. Later, both groups involved key staff members to participate in how the change would be implemented.
- Collaboration occurred in selected situations to recommend how the new organizational structure would be implemented. For instance, a group of employees worked with the leadership to develop the organization's vision statement, values, and promises. These were later shared with all employees for input.

- Empowerment has been the most challenging level of employee involvement. This change was mandated from the most senior levels of the University of North Texas System leadership. Empowerment has occurred in specific situations, however. The IT Shared Services operation, for example, has empowered a group of employees to identify and address opportunities to improve the culture and work experience. In addition, individual managers have been empowered to initiate continuous improvement projects.

THE CHALLENGE OF INVOLVEMENT

Participation, collaboration, and empowerment provide the greatest opportunities for involvement and buy-in. They also present the greatest challenges. Our experience with hundreds of clients has shown that leaders are most reluctant to fully utilize employee involvement in a change when the following beliefs exist:

- It takes too much time and will slow down the change.
- It takes too much work for the perceived value it will add.
- Others don't have the knowledge, competence, or experience to succeed.
- The scope of the change is small and the amount of resistance will be minimal—awareness and input are all we need.
- The leader doesn't want to lose or give up control.

Cynics will suggest that *any* reluctance comes down to a desire for control. That is often but not always the case.

WHEN NOT EVERYONE GETS TO PLAY

Involving everyone through participation, collaboration, and empowerment is impractical when dealing with large-scale change. Involving no one is a recipe for disaster.

The use of design or implementation teams has become standard practice for generating buy-in and support. They are useful the vast majority of the time. You can mess them up, however. A team to determine the course of action when the building is on fire is harmful not helpful.

It is also key to avoid setting the team up for failure by assembling a group that has no credibility with the frontline staff whose support you need.

Here are three rules of thumb:

1. Fill your team with people whom others will look at and say, "I know he [or she] will tell them the truth and make this work."
2. Provide the team with a clear charge, specific deliverables, and a visible sponsor to keep them on track and run interference for them.
3. The larger your change effort, the greater your commitment to awareness, input, and participation, even when everyone can't collaborate or be empowered.

LESSONS FROM THE NEW COKE

Has there ever been a bigger catastrophe when launching a product change than New Coke?

New Coke was supposed to be the answer to the legendary brand's declining market share. This wasn't change implemented on a whim. The company had seen its flagship product erode in its primary market for 15 years. Leaders had input from 200,000 people who said very clearly that they preferred the new formula to the traditional one.

Even so, the response to the release of New Coke was overwhelmingly bad. Calls on the company's customer hotline soared from 400 per day to more than 1,500 per day. Protest sprung up across the United States. Then–chief executive officer Roberto Goizueta even received a letter addressed "Chief Dodo, The Coca-Cola Company."

Goizueta called the decision to launch the New Coke "a prime example of taking intelligent risks" and considered that type of action critical for the company's ongoing success.[2]

The misstep by one of the most legendary brands in the world teaches us two important lessons about leading change:

1. Never underestimate the connection people have to a product, process, brand, or service and the impact of changing it.
2. Empowering others requires you to give up control.

DO YOU BELIEVE IN EMPOWERMENT?

The answer is virtually the same after years of asking that question. Everyone claims to believe in empowerment.

The application of that belief is another story.

Assume for a moment that you are the parent of a 10-year-old daughter. Tonight she greets you at the door with a request to accompany the 17-year-old boy from across town to a concert.

Wait for it. . . . There's more.

In his father's customized van.

Don't Freak Out

I'm not suggesting that anyone empower his or her 10-year-old daughter to choose whether she goes out with a 17-year-old boy. In fact, I would likely be the parent on the telephone to the local authorities if I were in that situation.

The point is that the concept of empowerment is easy. Actually empowering people to take intelligent risks is fraught with tough choices. The decision is easy if your 10-year-old wants to go out with a 17-year-old. It is more difficult if she wants to walk three doors down the street to visit her best friend from school.

Empowerment Is Giving Others Control

Parents of teenagers tell me that allowing their son or daughter to drive without adult supervision for the first time is a fearful experience—although one seminar participant did say that on the first evening his son left the house alone he went to bed at 8:30 and slept like a baby . . . he woke up every 2 hours and cried.

Leaders report a similar loss of control the first time they empower someone to make a change. There are four criteria that must be in place for successful empowerment. They won't make the fear go away, but they will help you minimize it.

1. Clarity around the mission, goal, and values
2. Appropriate knowledge and skills
3. Clear boundaries that provide opportunity for control within acceptable limits
4. The trust and freedom to fail in the honest pursuit of the mission and goal

The most important lessons we ever learn in life typically come from honest mistakes.

Not every change will be completely successful. Your willingness to involve others and use honest mistakes as learning opportunities—rather than occasions for public floggings—will build the trust and commitment you need to sustain a nimble organization that is always looking for opportunities to be faster, better, cheaper, and friendlier.

CHANGE LEADER ACTION LIST

1. Look for opportunities to involve people early and often. Make involvement part of your written change plans and make sure you use all five options whenever possible.
2. Look for more opportunities to give others control in the change process by empowering them. Start small if you just can't make yourself let go of the controls.
3. Remember, there are times when it is appropriate to empower people and there are times when awareness is all that is necessary. Be intentional about your actions to involve others. Just do it early and often.

Chapter 12

USE RESISTANCE AS YOUR FRIEND

People don't resist change. They resist being changed.

—Peter M. Senge

THERE IS ALWAYS AT LEAST ONE

Often there are several. You know . . . the ones who resist every change.

You have an image of them in your head right now, don't you?

If we are lucky, they adopt a neutral position to wait and see if the change has an opportunity to succeed. More likely, they will find the most inconvenient time to raise a question or make a comment that throws cold water on the group's enthusiasm.

My dear, sweet southern grandmother would have said that these are the people who would complain about a $100 gift . . . bless their heart.

WHAT WE WANT TO DO

Our initial reaction to resistance is emotion. They push us, and we want to push back. We might write off the first instance as the awkward execution of an honest attempt to offer a helpful insight. By the third time, we are dreading the change because we are certain that it will mean doing battle with "them."

Over the years, a few managers have even confessed to wanting to open their window, lean out, and scream the immortal line from the movie *Network:* "I'm mad as hell, and I'm not going to take it anymore!"

WHAT WE END UP DOING

You never really scream, do you?

I didn't think so. But chances are good that you have tried at least one—if not all—of the following approaches for dealing with resistance to change:

- *Reason with them.* You explain all the good business reasons why the change makes sense. They might listen. They might even agree with you. But they might counter with something so ludicrous that there is no rational response.
- *Bargain.* You offer them something in return. "If you support this, or at least not openly resist it, I will. . . ." Bargaining can buy you the support you need from that person or group, but the potential for negative reaction is huge if word gets out that you are bargaining for support.
- *Manipulate.* You attempt to manage the circumstances so that the resistors have no choice but to stay neutral or support the change. This is a high-stakes game that will result in even greater resistance and long-term mistrust not if but when it is discovered.
- *Use power.* You mandate compliance, and the result is malicious obedience. The resistance doesn't go away. It just becomes more difficult to detect.
- *Ignore.* You direct your energy toward the vast majority who support the change in hopes that the resistors go away. The problem is that many resistors respond to being ignored by talking louder.

AND THE WINNER IS . . .

The best opportunity is that your resistor is open to listening to reason. Beyond that, no one wins when you bargain, manipulate, use power, or ignore.

In fact, the resistance can get worse. People decide to:

- *Step up their resistance.* The Occupy and Tea Party movements in the United States are two examples of groups that increased their resistance when they felt disenfranchised and ignored.
- *Go underground.* Leonard Martin, the municipal government executive mentioned in Chapter 2, encountered staff members who attempted to do just the minimum when he announced that the culture of the organization would be changing. They

thought that he would either tire of the effort or leave for another job. Martin did neither, and over time, his team either supported the change or moved on. You can address underground resistance with enough patience and commitment.

- *Go guerilla.* Spreading rumors, undermining effort, and engaging in subtle sabotage are the tools of the guerilla resistor. Pilots for American Airlines were suspected of slowing down their effort to the point that it visibly hurt the company's performance and reputation in the fall of 2012. No proof could be offered, but the perception was that the pilots were undermining the company.

WE AREN'T FRUSTRATED BY REASONABLE PEOPLE

When it comes to resistance, we can work with those who listen to reason. Our first two courses of action for building support from the reasonable resistors should be to (1) solicit and understand their questions and concerns and (2) engage in a respectful conversation in which their concerns are addressed and the good business reasons for the change are discussed.

Remember the picture that popped into your head when I mentioned resistance at the beginning of the chapter? Were they reasonable people who ask logical questions in the attempt to understand the change and make it more successful?

Those were not the pictures in my head. The people who frustrate and even make me a little crazy are the unreasonable resistors who refuse to listen to reason.

WRAP YOUR MIND-SET AROUND THIS

Resistance is your friend. You don't have to celebrate or throw a party for it. But you should embrace the idea that resistance is natural. It allows you to identify potential barriers to making change work, and it increases your odds of building support.

If there is no resistance, there is no change.

THE QUESTIONS YOU MUST ANSWER

Do people want to be successful in their work, or do they want to be pains in the ass?

Most people want to be successful in their work. There might be a few who have become so jaded and disgruntled that they resist even the most beneficial of changes just because they want to make your life miserable. What percentage do you believe fall into that category? One to 2 percent? Five percent? Ten percent?

If the number is more than 10 percent, you have a different problem. You have serious culture and trust problems that need to be addressed. I suspect that the number is 5 percent or less. Here are two additional questions to answer:

1. Do you want to treat the 95 percent or more of good employees like the 5 percent or less who are out to sabotage your success?

or

2. Do you want to treat the 5 percent or less group like they are part of the 95 percent group until they give you proof that they are not a fit for your team?

The correct answer is number 2.

People want to feel as if their contributions matter. They will volunteer their commitment to leaders and organizations that engage their head and inspire their heart for a meaningful purpose.

THEIR RESISTANCE IS WELL INTENTIONED—NOW WHAT?

It may take some time to convince your resistors that you value their ideas and input. There may be years of mistrust and the perception that their ideas are not valued. Treating resistance with respect opens the door to open communication and improves problem solving. It also earns you more credibility if you have to tell the individual or group that their concerns cannot be addressed.

PULL: DON'T PUSH

"Why should I believe this change will be successfully implemented? The last one wasn't."

Bob wasn't sure how to respond. Monica was one of his most senior staff members, and she had a great deal of influence. The department was implementing a new automated medical records system, and he had hoped that the resistance would be minimal.

Rather than push back with the prepared talking points, Bob decided to pull.

"I'm not sure that I understand what you mean, Monica."

"Well, we're changing how we do things again after just a few years. Obviously, the last change didn't work."

Bob had the opening he needed. By using a question to pull Monica's concern to the surface, Bob was able to discuss the change in the context of the hospital's broader vision and strategic goals. He talked about how the last change was right for its time but that had been, as Monica said, a few years ago. A lot had changed in the health care world in that time.

Pushing back against resistance creates barriers. Using questions to pull the resistance out provides opportunity to create context.

What Is Most Important?

There are leaders who must have every activity accomplished in the precise way and at the exact time that they envisioned and approved on the change implementation plan. There are also those who are open to other implementation options as long as the purpose is achieved at the agreed-upon time and budget.

Which one are you?

The rigid leader who views resistance as a barrier that must be obliterated is more likely to find his or her change taken hostage by increased resistance, malicious obedience, or guerilla sabotage tactics.

Ronald Reagan said it well: "There is no limit to what a man can do or where he can go if he doesn't mind who gets the credit."

Involvement is an excellent tool for overcoming resistance.

SEVEN TACTICAL TIPS

How to address specific types of resistance is a question that frequently comes up in my presentations. Here are the seven that people tell me about most often and an idea for successfully addressing each.

1. **Know-It-Alls**

   Tries to impress with his or her knowledge and/or impose his or her will on the leader and group

   - Encourage others to comment on the individual's remarks.
   - In a group situation, ask others to either validate or repudiate the know-it-alls' statements. Pull the person aside, provide feedback, and ask for his or her help in involving others.
   - In a private situation, ask questions to determine the know-it-alls' level of expertise and then engage that person to help with the change as appropriate.

2. **Argumentative**

   Enjoys arguing over trivial details

   - Keep cool and make sure the participants do so as well.
   - Refocus the discussion on the broader goal and offer to have a one-on-one conversation to discuss his or her concerns.
   - Use questions to draw out the individual's true feelings and then get the opinion of the majority.
   - In a private situation, listen and then provide feedback about the behaviors that are creating the perception of being argumentative.

3. **Bad Attitude**

   Resents your position and thinks you are telling him or her how to do the job

   - Convince the individual that his or her experience is valuable to others.
   - Ask the person to share ideas about how to make the change work.
   - In private, provide feedback about behavior that is creating the perception of a bad attitude. The individual may not know how he or she is being perceived.

4. **Shy Clam**

   Does not participate or speak up; is passive-aggressive

   - Call on the person by name to give an opinion. You want to determine whether the individual is shy or being passive-aggressive in their resistance.
   - Ask a question that is likely to be answered well and then praise the individual.
   - Provide a specific assignment related to the change if appropriate.

5. **Skeptic**

Finds reasons why every idea cannot be successfully implemented

- Acknowledge that there are always challenges in implementing any change.
- Ask the individual's ideas on how to overcome the obstacles he or she has presented.
- Establish a guiding principle that every barrier must be accompanied by a potential solution.

6. **Grudge Carrier**

Hangs on to something in the past that didn't go his or her way

- Avoid discussion about the person's pet peeve.
- Explain the appropriate place for addressing his or her issue if it is not relevant to the discussion.
- In a group setting, indicate that the individual's issue will be captured and addressed at a later time.

7. **Group Favorite**

Is wrong, but others in the group will not correct out of respect

- Avoid direct criticism, sarcasm, and ridicule.
- Try to discuss issues without referring to the individual specifically.
- Talk with him or her privately about specific situations.

CHANGE LEADER ACTION LIST

1. The mind-set that the resistance you experience is rooted in a desire to succeed, a concern about success, or, at worst, a conflicting agenda is critical. An initial approach to resistance that assumes the best increases your success.
2. Planning and preparation are critical for addressing resistance. Make sure you allow time to identify the usual resistance suspects and the statements that you expect from them. Think through the statements or questions you expect and then prepare your responses in advance.

(*continued*)

(*continued*)

3. Practice pulling ideas out of people rather than pushing back in the face of resistance. You can refine this technique in nonchange situations, such as asking for extra input in staff meetings or coaching sessions.

4. There will be times when you must be the leader. When strategies for successfully engaging others have not worked, move forward knowing that you made an honest attempt to use resistance as your friend.

Part III

CHANGE CHALLENGES

Chapter 13

WHEN CHANGE ISN'T A CHOICE

Any change, any loss, does not make us victims. Others can shake you, surprise you, disappoint you, but they can't prevent you from acting, from taking the situation you're presented with and moving on.

—Blaine Lee

"IT'S NOT PERSONAL; IT'S JUST BUSINESS"

That's what they say when they want to ease the pain of delivering bad news, right?

Guess what? It doesn't work . . . at least not at the time.

Bill Spence was my favorite boss of all time.[1] I reported to him for three and a half years while working at the diamond drill bit company I mentioned in Chapter 9. I would have worked for Bill longer except the company was sold and moving to Houston, Texas.

I knew that I wouldn't move with the plant. I was an hourly employee working afternoons and evenings in shipping while completing my degree. Even so, the Friday afternoon conversation I had with Bill the day that would be my last day caught me off guard.

Have you noticed that unexpected life events are never preceded by a memo saying, "Tomorrow you will experience a difficult change. Get ready"?

IT REALLY WAS JUST BUSINESS

Bill's conversation was professional and to the point: "You know that we are moving the plant in a few months, and we know that you aren't planning to go with us. We've decided to let you go now rather than keep you on through the transition. Thank you for being a great employee. I've enjoyed working with you."

The decision to let me go came about six months earlier than expected. My first feeling was apprehension: I would need to find another job. Fortunately, it didn't take long to recover.

In the grand scheme of loss, this was an easy one. I have had more challenging setbacks in my career. So have you. That's the point. This was change that I knew would come at some point delivered by a boss whom I respected. And there was still a momentary feeling of setback and loss.

Imagine how you feel when it is something really serious.

THE ONE THING THAT MATTERS MOST

My feelings had nothing to do with Bill's presentation or intent. It really wasn't personal. It *was* just business.

I made it personal through my perceptions about the situation and my disrupted expectations. I chose my response. You do, too, and so do the members of your team when they are confronted with change that isn't a choice.

As a teacher and therapist, Dr. Jack Pennington (yes, my brother) has spent decades helping individuals make sense of situations in their lives. He explains the importance of taking responsibility for your own perceptions this way:

> Each person is the thinker of his own thoughts and, thus, the architect of his own experiences or understanding of what he calls reality or "the situation." So rather than life events or circumstance determining how they respond in any given situation, the quality of their functioning can be traced to their thinking process and the degree to which they recognize their thinking in the moment.

Our thoughts are translated to feeling so quickly that we aren't aware of them. Past experience influences our thinking and perception, but so do a lot of other factors, such as our confidence in the future and the belief in our ability to respond in a positive manner.

The most important thing we can do when change isn't a choice is to recognize that our feelings reflect our thinking. Listening to our feelings as indicators of our thoughts helps us take responsibility for our behavior in the face of change.

STOP READING FOR A MOMENT

We all face change that is out of our control at some point. You can view it as a setback, a disappointment, or an opportunity.

You can call your response being resilient, bouncing back, or taking advantage of the situation. What you call it doesn't matter. What matters is your ability to keep moving forward and thrive. How we feel in every situation is determined by how we think about what is happening.

Our task as individuals is to take responsibility for how we think about and ultimately respond to situations that are out of our control. Our job as leaders is to help others do the same.

LET'S GET PERSONAL

How do you respond to change that is outside of your control? Do you consciously think about the reality you could create? Or do you allow circumstances—more specifically the perception you have assigned to those circumstances—to dictate your response?

Ideally, we would all look toward what is possible in the future rather than allowing the past to interpret the present. Dwelling on the present through a destructive lens of past perception does little to help us make proactive, responsible choices about how to respond today.

Most people, however, are very good at doing the thing that most keeps them from a positive response to change—they allow past perception to define how they respond today. There is an adage that past performance is the best predictor of future performance. That happens because most of us are not very good at thinking clearly about the opportunities presented by change.

SO WHAT DO I DO?

Breaking old—often lifelong—patterns of how you think about change is extremely difficult. The most important things you can do right now are:

- *Slow down and think to separate emotion from response.* Make a conscious choice to think from the perspective of how you want to respond rather than how your emotions have conditioned you to respond.
- *Acknowledge reality.* Dan O'Brien and Dave Johnson were locked in what was to be a highly publicized battle for the gold medal in the Decathlon at the 1992 Olympic Games in Barcelona. That changed when O'Brien failed to qualify for the team.

O'Brien said, "I remember feeling really alone, with nobody to turn to."[2] Sadness, anger, and confusion are responses that extend from our thinking. Acknowledging our feelings as representative of our current thinking is a first step. Using that understanding to reframe our thinking is true progress.

- *Recognize the challenges.* In these days of instant everything, it is important to remember that a quick decision to move forward doesn't minimize the time and effort of doing so.

- *Take stock.* There is a tendency to feel that everything changes when one aspect of our life changes. Make a list of the things that have and have not changed. Define what is over and what isn't. An objective look at your resources, options, and reality can help set the stage for positive action.

- *Explore a different future.* We often define ourselves by our past rather than our potential. Arthritis prevented Anna Mary Robertson Moses from doing the needlework she loved, so she began painting at age 75. Twenty-six years and approximately 1,600 paintings later, Grandma Moses had become one of America's most acclaimed artists. Take the opportunity to ask new questions that will lead to unique opportunities.

- *Take baby steps.* Many people thought television personality Deborah Norville was washed up at age 33. She had risen almost overnight to become cohost of NBC's *Today* show, and, just as quickly, she was gone. Norville became depressed and nonfunctional. Her first step toward regaining control was choosing to get out of bed and take a shower. One shower led to the resolve to do it every day. That turned into getting dressed and going outside. A yearlong stint in radio provided the confidence to retry television, which ultimately led to a revitalized career.[3] As the adage goes, "How does an ant eat an elephant? One bite at a time."

- *Celebrate success.* We celebrate birthdays, anniversaries, the end of the year, and retirement. So here's the question: Why wait? Look for every opportunity to celebrate behavior that represents new thinking and moves you toward your new beginning.

BACK TO BUSINESS

Pam was struggling to stay positive. The company was changing its employee health plan, and it would cost those with dependent coverage much more money than the small pay raises would cover.

Pam's job as vice president of human resources required her to occasionally deliver bad news, but this time it was different. It was a change with which she did not agree. She was a single parent herself and believed that others would find it difficult to absorb the extra costs. Pam had lobbied hard with her colleagues on the executive team to make a different decision. But she lost.

Pam confessed:

> I have a hard time accepting things that I cannot control; that is especially true when I do not believe that it is a good change. My emotions show on my face, and I know that employees will be able to tell that I am not in agreement. And I don't know what I am going to say if someone asks me what I think of this change. I don't want to lie to anyone, but I'm not sure that I can simply repeat the company line.

YOUR JOB AS THE LEADER

Pam's dilemma is common. You will be asked to communicate and implement changes that you did not make and with which you may not agree.

If the course of action you are being asked to take is illegal, unethical, or immoral, bring it to the appropriate person's attention. If the change is so abhorrent that you cannot in good conscience support the organization's decision, consider removing yourself from that situation. If you—like Pam—have clearly communicated your position and did not get your way, do what you are expected to do. Supporting the organization's goals and decisions is part of your job.

THE QUESTION IS, "HOW?"

How you communicate in these situations presents an opportunity to help others move more quickly and positively past their disrupted expectations. Here are six tips to use when formulating and delivering your message:

1. *Focus on the facts.* Tell others what the change is and how it affects them. Now is not the time to embed your feelings about the situation into the discussion. And whatever you do, avoid phrases such as, "This hurts me more than it does you." The people receiving the message will not really believe it or care.

2. *Acknowledge the truth, and don't throw others under the bus.* People want to know how the change is going to affect them. If it sucks, admit it. You don't have to be brutal, but you must be honest. Don't blame others or point fingers. Doing so destroys your credibility and sabotages the organization.

3. *Listen and understand without agreeing.* It is okay to allow some time for venting. Questions and frustration are common when expectations are disrupted. It can even help lower the emotions and create the space to help others refocus on how they think about the change. Just be sure to maintain your public support for the decision. Saying, "I understand how you can feel this way," is okay. Saying, "I agree with you, but this is coming from the senior leaders," is not.

4. *Focus others on what they can control whenever and wherever you can.* Remember that people support what they help create, and we all want to exercise control in our lives. Look for places where others can exercise at least some control over how the change is implemented. The one thing that we can all control is how we think and respond when faced with difficult situations. Remind them that they have choices about how they move forward.

5. *Create the expectation for the future.* Let others know what they can expect from you and what you expect from them regarding the change. At a minimum, others should know how communication around the change will be addressed. They should also hear you express confidence that they will respond to the change in the most positive, professional manner possible.

6. *Seek, suggest, or offer help if appropriate.* Pam sought help in formulating her message because she wanted to honor her responsibility to the company. You should do the same. Suggesting or offering help to others should also be an option. Your human resources and employee assistance program team are excellent resources. If those are not available, look around your organization or community for places to which you can refer people for help as they work through traumatic change.

A QUICK POINT ON TERMINATING EMPLOYMENT

Many managers have told me that telling someone that his or her employment is being terminated or his or her job is being eliminated is one of the most difficult conversations they are called on to conduct. The general tips we just discussed apply in these situations as well, but remember that laws and policies governing what you can and cannot say vary. Be sure to follow the requirements that apply to your organization and location.

HOW COULD YOU SUPPORT THIS?

That is the question Pam feared most. She had, in hindsight, made statements that she knew would be thrown back in her face. There would be people in the audience who knew of her personal situation and feelings. They might not put her on the spot in public, but they would certainly do so in private.

Pam wanted to be loyal to the company, and she feared her credibility would suffer. Her thinking was that anything less than 100 percent consistency with her stated views would cause others to question her integrity.

The best response would not be easy for her. Here is the counsel I provided:

> This decision was a difficult one. I shared my views, and others shared theirs. After thoughtful consideration, the leadership team made a decision to pursue this course of action. I support that decision and am working to make sure that we implement it to the best of our ability.

DON'T LET THEM SUCK YOU IN

There will be follow-up questions. You can probably hear them already: "Do you really support this? Do you think it will work? Did they change your mind?"

Remember, you are a leader in an organization. You are not a candidate in a popularity contest. You don't have to justify your decision to support the leadership team's decision.

IT IS ABOUT LEADERSHIP

Napoleon Bonaparte said, "A leader is a dealer in hope."

We do not always get to choose what happens. We do choose how we think about it, how we handle it, and how we help others do so.

In the end, may we all echo the words of Grandma Moses: "I look back on my life a good day's work, it was done and I feel satisfied with it. I made the best out of what life offered."

CHANGE LEADER ACTION LIST

1. Identify the thoughts that are driving your perceptions, feelings, and emotions about change. Our thinking drives our feelings, not the other way around. Determine where you need to take responsibility for changing how you think.

2. Create your personal plan for dealing with the change based on the ideas offered in this chapter. Others are watching, and they will find strength in your resiliency and example.

3. Create a detailed plan for your communication to others. You can find a checklist to help you gather your thoughts in the Resources section at www.pennington group.com/make-change-work/.

4. Invest in increasing your credibility now. My conversation with Bill Spence was easier to accept because of the relationship he had created with me over the previous three and a half years.

Chapter 14

CHANGE YOUR CULTURE AND CHANGE YOUR RESULTS

Everything you do to try to adapt and change and renew a company—whether it's organizational change, marketing, finance, HR—takes place in a crucible and that crucible is culture.

—Louis V. Gertsner, Jr.

THE BEST AND THE REST

What separates the marketplace heroes from the has-beens and wanna-bes?

It can't be only products, services, or price. There is competition everywhere. And yet there are businesses, government agencies, and nonprofits that don't just compete with the others; they dominate in areas such as product and service quality, innovation, execution, and, most important, results.

Your competitors don't hire all geniuses and leave you with the dunces. Their computer systems, compensation, and operational processes are not dramatically different from yours. When they discuss strategy, the words on their flip charts are not significantly more insightful than yours. The difference is, ultimately, an intangible. It is a culture where every person at every level is focused on and committed to doing whatever it takes—including readily embracing change—to deliver meaningful results.

That's your primary leadership job: to build a compelling culture that becomes the intangible that sets your organization apart.

WHY TALK ABOUT CULTURE IN A BOOK ABOUT CHANGE?

We have known about the importance of organizational culture for decades. Yet the role your culture plays in making change work and achieving long-term success has never been more crucial. Here's why:

- *Culture beats strategy.* Southwest Airlines is not the only airline to adopt a low-cost strategy to compete in its marketplace.

127

It is simply the best at creating a culture where everyone is totally committed to implementing that strategy. If your strategy is not supported by your culture, your culture always wins.

- *Culture beats change.* Early in my professional career I worked in state government. The newly elected governor ran on a platform of streamlining and cutting employment. Four years later, the size of government had grown at about the same rate that it had before he took office. The rhetoric changed, but the culture remained the same. In a battle between sustaining change and the existing culture, place your bets on the culture.

- *Culture serves as an anchor or accelerator for change.* Everyone talks about a desire for continuous innovation. USAA, the award-winning financial services company serving individuals who have served in the US military and their families, takes it to an entirely different level. This is the company that first introduced check depositing through photos taken by a smartphone.

  At USAA, innovation is encouraged and expected from everyone, and the numbers indicate this has been a success: 8,000 ideas, a 95 percent participation rate in innovation, and 247 new patents in 2012.[1] The company's commitment to creating and sustaining the culture serves as the accelerator that separates it from all the companies that talk about innovation and never deliver.

- *Culture attracts talent, and talent affects your ability to be nimble and resilient.* Talented people have a choice. The companies that are consistently beating you in the marketplace are creating environments where talented people appreciate the opportunity to contribute and succeed. They take the extra time to hire for fit. And they think in terms of talent development rather than performance management. You might score the occasional upset without a culture that attracts and nurtures talented people, but consistent excellence will be difficult to sustain.

CULTURE: WHAT IT IS AND WHAT IT ISN'T

The MSN Encarta Dictionary defines *culture* as "the patterns of behavior and thinking that people living in social groups learn, create, and share." Culture isn't the holiday party or monthly birth-day celebration. It isn't casual dress on Fridays, and it isn't sched-uled fun on a quarterly basis.

There is nothing wrong with any of these activities. When done as part of the natural way things are done because of shared beliefs and values, they are fine examples of the culture—although I can make a strong case that scheduled fun is an oxymoron that hurts more than it helps.

Culture is the DNA of your business that defines the "way we do things around here." It is the integrated patterns of human behav-ior that include thought, speech, and action. Culture is the security guard at USAA who excels at contributing innovation ideas. It is the ground crew at Southwest Airlines that puts in extra effort to maintain turnaround times in the face of a snowstorm and sub-freezing temperatures. And yes, it is the fun atmosphere at Zappos that contributes to excellent customer service rather than detracts from it.

In short, culture is the habits your organization displays over time that show what you truly believe about your purpose, people, performance, and professionalism. Those habits are defined and driven by shared:

- Purpose
- Values, assumptions, beliefs
- Performance expectations and standards
- Language, legends, and symbols

THE CHALLENGE OF CULTURE CHANGE

What companies come to mind when you think of legendary cul-tures and great place to work? Three of the names I hear often have already been mentioned in this chapter: Southwest Airlines, Zappos, and USAA. The following national names are usually mixed in with a number of lesser known but equally great cultures when the question is asked in my presentations:

- Google
- Nordstrom
- Les Schwab Tire Centers
- Publix

- Whole Foods
- DSW Shoes
- Procter & Gamble

One common factor jumps out as I review these legendary organizations: They focused on culture from their beginning rather than completing a cultural overhaul later after missteps.

That doesn't mean that you can't change your organization's or team's culture. But transforming a culture is the most challenging type of change in which you can engage.

HOW HARD IS IT?

Asking how difficult it will be is a little like asking, "How long and hard must you train to complete a marathon?"

There is one answer if you are in great health, are in excellent physical condition, and regularly run long distances. There is another completely different answer if the only two times you ever consider running is (1) if you are being chased by a robber or (2) if you have to go to the bathroom really bad.

So let's assume that the one word that best describes your culture is *mediocre*. You can expect to devote two to three years of consistent attention to this change . . . and that is *if* you devote adequate resources to the challenge.

WHY IS IT SO DIFFICULT?

Creating a new culture requires developing and building buy-in for a common set of unifying values, assumptions, beliefs, and habits that drive actionable performance and behavior toward a shared purpose.

You will need every leadership skill covered in this book to overcome the baggage and create the buy-in to begin this change. Even then, it will be a difficult challenge. Here's why:

- There is a great deal of baggage to unload. People come to a new company wanting to succeed. They are willing to give you the benefit of the doubt if only because they want to keep their new job. In a change effort, you must deal with years or even decades of mistrust and failed change efforts masquerading as the voice of experience within your team.

- It takes a long time to develop new habits. Traditional wisdom says that it takes 21 days to develop a new habit. My experience is different. For instance, I read that eating a small amount of dark chocolate every day is good for your health. I tried the 72 percent cocoa solids version and immediately developed the habit. But well after 21 days, I still struggle at blogging as much as I would like.

  Habit formation is driven by a number of factors, including the strength of the urge to change and the reinforcement you receive from doing so. Researchers at the University College London report that although their best estimate is 60 days, their studies have shown new habits forming in as few as 18 days and as many as 254.[2] Now multiply that by the number of people who you need to get on board for the new culture, and the challenge becomes obvious.

- Everything affects the culture, and the culture affects everything. The quote from former IBM chief executive officer Louis Gerstner, Jr., at the beginning of this chapter sums up the problem. The culture that you are trying to create is engaged in conflict with the one that currently exists. Every new idea, action, and change is being affected by the existing culture. Imagine competing viruses in your body, and you start to get the picture.

- Results are not immediate, so people lose interest. You might see some immediate improvements, but it will be months before you notice significant change. Think of it like your new exercise program: You have to put in weeks and months of effort before people on the outside notice a significant difference. Improvements start happening much sooner, but it is easy to lose focus when they are not readily visible at the outset.

SEVEN IMPERATIVES

There is no 10- or 12-step program for changing a culture. There are, however, seven critical imperatives that must be accomplished to achieve buy-in and develop new habits.

1. *Define the purpose, vision, values, and current reality.* You can't simply say, "The culture needs to change." You must clearly define how the future must be different from the present.

2. *Create continual awareness.* About the time that you believe you have sent every imaginable message about the importance of the culture, you are beginning to cut through the clutter of workplace distractions.

3. *Cultivate the language.* Words have meaning. We're not talking a cult-like, secret ceremony language. The best cultures adopt and cultivate the language of success rather than of failure.

4. *Leverage the legends and symbols.* Promotions, salary increases, and recognition are the symbols of success in organizations. Use them wisely to reinforce behavior that is aligned with your desired culture. Create and share the legends of performance that demonstrate the culture in action.

5. *Build and maintain the competencies.* Desire to live the culture without the knowledge and skills to do so creates frustration and causes others to doubt your commitment to the change.

6. *Align structure, process, and procedure.* Structure, process, and procedure create habits. Make sure that the habits you create support the values, beliefs, assumptions, and aspirations of your culture.

7. *Actively assimilate and strengthen group membership.* Hire for fit. Teach new team members your culture through an intentional on-boarding process. Coach for cultural fit as well as performance, and be willing to remove those who do not live your values—even if they produce good results.

CHANGE LEADER ACTION LIST

Leaders who develop great cultures make different choices than their competitors in every area of the business. As a result, they don't simply compete—they dominate their markets. Here are three things to do now:

1. Assess your current culture. Is it an anchor holding you back or an accelerator pushing your forward? You can find an assessment tool in the Resources section at www.penningtongroup.com/make-change-work/.
2. Look for areas to utilize the seven levers for driving culture change covered in this chapter. You can download thought starter ideas in the resource section at www.penningtongroup.com/make-change-work/.
3. Show the courage of accountability. It is not enough to simply state the purpose, goals, and values. You must actively define and demonstrate what they look like in practice and create the environment for change to occur. There is a line from the often-quoted "Unknown" that applies here: "If you really want to do something, you will find a way; if you don't, you'll find an excuse."

Chapter 15

STOP SPINEATING

The 3 Cs of life: choices, chances, and changes. You must make a choice to take a chance or your life will never change.

—Unknown

HOW I GAINED 70 POUNDS

I made a big change after my junior year in high school. Actually, I changed to become big.

The end of my junior year found me standing 6 feet tall and weighing 145 pounds. My high school graduation found me 1 inch taller and weighing 185 pounds. Five years later, I had added another 30 pounds and was out of college and in my first professional job.

I looked like Mister Potato Head—all body and skinny legs. There were two reasons for my weight gain. The first 20 to 25 pounds were biological as I filled out my skinny teenage body. The last 45 to 50 pounds were behavioral. In short, I stopped playing basketball and running a gazillion miles every week and kept eating as if I was still playing. Add late-night trips to the local pizza place while I was in college, and the freshman 15 became the Bachelor's degree 30.

IT IS BEHAVIORAL CONDITIONING

We taught mice and pigeons to do all sorts of interesting things during my graduate school class in behavioral psychology. The principle is simple: provide a stimulus and elicit a response. The stimulus-response cycle still plays an important role in animal training today. Your pet dog goes outside to take care of his biological business, and you say, "Good boy!" He goes inside on the floor, and you scold, "Bad dog!"

IT WORKS WITH PEOPLE, TOO

Stimulus-response is evident in child rearing. Parents instinctively swat the hand and yell, "No!" if they catch their child about to touch a hot stove. If the child touches the stove, the resulting heat will teach him or her that grabbing something hot is painful and dangerous. It is simple stimulus-response.

As we get older, this pattern of behavior stays with us. Do you instinctively let the driver who cuts you off in traffic know that he or she is enemy number one in your eyes? Are you selective about the finger you use to send that message?

How about holiday gatherings with family? Do you find yourself responding the same way every time your least favorite relative brings up that embarrassing story from your youth or makes a political statement with which you disagree?

You don't think about your response; you just make it. And at some point, it becomes automatic.

SPINEATING (SPINE-ATING)

The late Dr. Murlon Dye, one of my graduate school professors, coined the term *spineating* to describe the human tendency to respond without thinking. It is a destructive stimulus-response loop that causes us to react in ways that are often not in our best interest. Here's how it works:

> A stimulus hits us and then travels up the nervous system to our spinal cord. Rather than continuing to the brain, where it can be processed, the stimulus takes a 90-degree turn at a point parallel to our mouth and the response blurts out with no evidence of thought.

Spineating is, of course, physically impossible. But we have all seen and experienced people responding to situations in ways that make the concept seem plausible.

ORGANIZATIONAL SPINEATING

The tendency to fall into destructive stimulus-response loops is equally evident in organizations and teams. It is one of the most difficult challenges we face in making change work.

In times of financial crisis, spineating can cause organizations to make indiscriminate cuts that ultimately do more harm than good. In our efforts to implement change or transform the organization, it can chain us to past perception rather than empower us to be future-focused.

On a more practical level, you can see evidence of this destructive stimulus-response loop in the following:

- The team member who automatically responds that the leader cannot be trusted when even the slightest piece of information is withheld—and even if there was a completely legitimate reason for doing so
- The leader who automatically considers even legitimate questions as a personal affront and labels the offending employee as a troublemaker who must be punished
- The customer service person who makes life miserable for every customer who happens to complain, giving no apparent thought to the impact of this behavior on the organization's reputation

HOW I LOST 50 POUNDS

There was a day that I decided that I didn't want to die of a heart attack before the age of 40. There was no medical emergency that precipitated this thought. It simply came to me. I knew that I needed to change my behavior and that doing so would require me to do three things:

1. Break the stimulus-response loop that caused me to devour any snack food that was in front of me when I was bored.
2. Consume fewer calories than I burned on any given day.
3. Commit to an exercise program.

The exercise program was a matter of discipline. The munchies were a bigger challenge.

THE RUBBER BAND MAN

My answer came in the form of a rubber band worn around my wrist. Its inconspicuous presence tucked behind my watch on my left arm gave me something benign to do with my hands when food was present. Most important, its presence helped keep me in the moment so that I could make a choice that took me in the direction I wanted to go rather than continuing to repeat old mistakes.

BREAKING THE SPINEATING HABIT IN ORGANIZATIONS

Wouldn't it be great if the solution to transforming your organization would be to give everyone a rubber band? Actually, organizations do a version of that all the time. They put posters on the wall, load screen savers on their computer screens, and even distribute those little rubber wristbands. They hold contests and implement recognition programs. And they actively use the seven levers we discussed in Chapter 14 to build and sustain a culture.

WHERE IT BREAKS DOWN

Those external attempts to remind people of the desired future break down when there is no internal buy-in to the vision. The physical reinforcement comes across as a gimmick or manipulation.

PURSUE THE BEST OVER THE EASIEST

I introduced readers to Carl Sewell and Sewell Automotive Companies in my book *Results Rule!* Sewell's Lexus and Cadillac dealerships are perennially at or near the top in service and sales in the United States.

Sewell told me that the decision to be the best was the most important business decision that his company ever made. That decision made life simpler, more profitable, and more fun[1].

The goal for all organizations that want to stay nimble and relevant in today's marketplace is to understand what being the best means for them and to consciously choose that path rather than doing what is easy. For Sewell, being the best means service. For Apple, it means being innovative. For Walmart, it means being the low-cost provider. Your choice may be different. The only thing that matters is that your choice be based on what the customer values and what will help you win in the marketplace.

Today, Sewell's decision to be the best is part of his company's culture. In the beginning, he and the rest of the company had to actively pursue it rather than fall back into their old responses. Doing what you have always done is easy. All you have to do is fall into the spineating trap. Doing the best takes work.

CHANGE LEADER ACTION LIST

1. Ensure absolute clarity on the vision and what it means for every level of the organization. This sounds obvious, but it is a place where change efforts succumb to doing what is easy rather than what is best. There is clarity for the vision at the top level, and then the message morphs and changes as it cascades throughout the organization.

   The senior IT leaders at one of my national insurance clients saw the potential for their message about their new culture to become fractured as it moved through their multiple locations and teams. Their response was to have the five senior leaders conduct the education sessions on the new culture so that everyone heard the same vision. Then they engaged employees at all levels in the discussion about what the new culture meant for them to build buy-in and support.

2. Teach people how their thinking—or lack of it—affects their ability to respond to and implement change. The opposite of spineating is purposeful action based on an internalized vision for the future. Most of us are unaware of how we respond based out of habit rather than conscious thought.

3. Create cues that cause you to think. What is your version of the rubber band? You are looking for something that will make you slow down to consider whether what you are doing is the best action or simply the easy approach.

4. Make it safe and worthwhile for others to help you to break the unconscious stimulus-response loop. Getting employees to tell a leader the truth is one of the most

(continued)

(*continued*)

difficult challenges any organization faces. The IT leaders at my insurance client make a conscious commitment to informal skip-level meetings designed to ensure that they are hearing the truth. Sewell gives everyone permission to call him at any time to discuss a concern. Opening the door is the easy part. Pursuing the best means that you must make it safe for people to actually walk through it and say what is on their mind.

Part IV

THE WRAP-UP

Chapter 16

THE FUTURE AND CHANGE

It is not the strongest of the species that survives, nor the most intelligent, but the one most responsive to change.

—Charles Darwin

NO WONDER WE FEEL OVERWHELMED

Back in 2006, the people at IBM Global Technology Services predicted that by 2010, the world's information base would be doubling every 11 hours.[1] It is uncertain if the authors of this paper factored in the creation of YouTube in late 2005 and the proliferation of pet, young child, and stupid people tricks videos. If not, the available information in the world might have doubled in the few hours that it took you to read this book.

INFORMATION DOES NOT EQUAL CHANGE

A wealth of information is no guarantee that anything will change. Companies continue to bungle change efforts, treat employees poorly, and make bad choices about their strategy despite a never-ending supply of books, articles, and presentations.

We have yet to solve the problems of homelessness or significantly upgrade the overall quality of public education in the United States despite numerous studies suggesting solutions. We don't even actively engage in efforts to change when we have ample information and a desire to do so. The Gallup organization reported that only 10 percent of Americans approved of the job the US Congress was doing in August 2012—less than 90 days before the 2012 general election.[2] With that level of, hopefully, informed disapproval, you might reasonably expect voters to demand a wholesale change. After all, there was no shortage of information about why candidates think they deserve your support.

The facts tell a different story about how our apparent desire for change translates to action. All 435 seats in the US House of Representatives were up for election. An amazing 92.8 percent of incumbents who ran were reelected (93.8 percent of Democrats and 92.1 percent of Republicans).[3]

FOCUS ON WHAT YOU KNOW AND CAN PREDICT

Too much information can add to our feelings of being over-whelmed. You are familiar with that phenomenon if you have found yourself facing several hundred alternatives in the shampoo aisle of your local grocery store and wondering which one to pick.

Futurist Daniel Burrus believes that we can anticipate many, if not most, of the changes on our horizon by focusing on certainty and basing our strategies on that information. He says: "We know a great deal more about the future than we think we know. We just need to understand where to look."[4]

Here are five trends we know will drive the changes you need to succeed in the future:

1. *Customer expectations will continue to increase.* Today's "WOW!" experience will become tomorrow's "Been there; done that." You must continue to meet customers' fundamental expec-tations and be distinctive in ways that add value. It isn't an either/or decision. Both are required.
2. *Keeping the best and brightest talent means that you must change how you engage your workforce.* Timeless values and principles such as respect, appreciation, and empowerment will remain. How you demonstrate them will change.
3. *Technology will become smaller, more personal, and increasingly video-driven.* Two studies by the Pew Research Center point the direction for the future:
   - Seventy-eight percent of all teens have a cell phone, and 37 percent of teens have a smartphone. One in four teens considers themselves to be cell-only Internet users.[5]
   - Ninety-five percent of teens use the Internet. Thirty-seven percent of them use video chat applications such as Skype, Google Talk, or iChat.[6]

These developments will change how you market to and interact with customers, as well as how work is accomplished.

4. *We will continue to age.* In the United States, the number of adults aged 65 and older is expected to double between 2009 and 2050.[7] Life span projections from around the world are expected to continue to increase. The profound impact of an aging population on health care is already being anticipated. The effect on employment, new business development, and technology continues to evolve.

5. *Cost containment will not go out of style.* We may eventually return to the free-spending days of the recent past, but our history with the financial trauma of the Great Depression in the 1930s suggest that people and companies will be careful and more discriminating with what and where they spend.

TWO ENDURING TRUTHS ABOUT SUCCESSFUL CHANGE

Making change work will always be about connecting with people, bringing them together, and keeping them focused on a common purpose. Trends point the direction. Technology opens new opportunities. But those are simply interesting ideas until people make them work.

As long as people are essential to change, leaders who can make change work will be in constant demand.

HOW YOU CAN WIN

One of Jack Welch's most astute comments as chief executive officer of General Electric still applies today:[8]

> The difference between winning and losing will be how the men and women of our company view change as it comes at them. If they see it as a threat—as an ill wind to be resisted by keeping your head down and digging your feet in—we lose. But if they are provided the educational tools and encouraged to use them—to the point where they see change as synonymous with opportunity, where they become receptive to it, even demand it—then every door we must pass through to win big all around the world will swing open to us.

Here's how you win:

1. *Embrace the coyote and run from becoming a dodo.* Not literally, of course. Coyotes don't really enjoy being embraced by humans, and you probably could never get them to agree to it without risking serious injury. And dodos are extinct, so that's not really possible either.

   You can, however, learn from the traits of both the dodo and the coyote and apply them to stay nimble, relevant, and engaged. Now is a good time to revisit the survey in Chapter 4.

   As a reminder, the dodo bird:
   - Grew up in a stable, secure environment with no need to worry about predators or outside danger.
   - Lost the ability to expand its reach because of comfort and complacency.
   - Had no ability to distinguish predators from friends.
   - Lost or never developed the ability to adapt quickly to changing opportunities or threats (primary and secondary).
   - Never saw change coming or anticipated a different possible future, leaving itself with no time to adapt.

   On the other hand, coyotes are known as:
   - Being opportunistic problem solvers with the willingness to adapt.
   - Possessing excellent vision and sense of smell.
   - Being speedy.
   - Valuing strong family groups that take care of their young.
   - Being versatile and willing to work alone, in teams, and even with other animals to succeed.

2. *Don't confuse the tool with the goal.* One client described his organization as in search of the next BSO—bright shiny object. It is easy to fall in love with the tool as the next sexy change initiative. New tools help you know what you can do. Clear goals and purpose keep you focused on what you should do.

3. *Make change a strategic advantage.* The landscape is littered with companies that became complacent and irrelevant. They forgot to sustain a culture that relentlessly focuses on customers, continually increases operational excellence, and creates an environment where talented people want to help you succeed.

ONE FINAL THOUGHT

People want to be led through change, not managed through it. They want to contribute to exciting work that achieves a meaningful result for the customers they serve. They want to make change work, and they want you to lead them.

Show your resolve and demonstrate your resilience. Hold on to your enthusiasm and commitment. Most important, accept the responsibility.

You can do this.

NOTES

PREFACE

1. John P. Kotter, "Leading Change: Why Transformation Efforts Fail," *Harvard Business Review* (March–April 1995): 1.

CHAPTER 2   FASTER, BETTER, CHEAPER, FRIENDLIER

1. Joe Calloway, *Becoming a Category of One* (Hoboken, NJ: John Wiley & Sons, 2009), 140.

2. Ibid., 141.

3. Kevin Kelly, "Better Than Human," *Wired* (January 2013).

CHAPTER 3   GOOD CHANGE, BAD CHANGE

1. William Bridges, *Managing Transitions* (New York: Addison-Wesley, 1991), 3.

CHAPTER 4   DODOS AND COYOTES: ONLY THE NIMBLE SURVIVE

1. Richard Bach, *Jonathan Livingston Seagull* (New York: Scribner, 1998).

2. You can find a great deal of information about the dodo bird at www.thejunglestore.com/Dodos and www.wild-facts.com/tag/dodo-bird-facts/.

3. The *Road Runner* cartoons were created by animation director Chuck Jones for Warner Brothers in 1948. The template for the stories was created by writer Michael Maltese.

http://en.wikipedia.org/wiki/Wile_E._Coyote_and_The_Road_Runner and http://kevinmccorrytv.webs.com/rrshow.htm.

4. You can find a great deal of information about coyotes at http://animals.nationalgeographic.com/animals/mammals/coyote/.

5. Amy Briggs, "Coyotes Not Only Wily, They're Also Faithful," *National Geographic Tales of the Weird* (October 2, 2012), http://newswatch.nationalgeographic.com/2012/10/02/coyotes-not-only-wily-theyre-also-faithful/.

6. Ibid.

7. Cristen Conger, "Do Coyotes and Badgers Work Together to Find Food?" http://animal.discovery.com/animal-facts/coyotes-badgers-find-food1.htm.

CHAPTER 8   CHANGE CHANGE

1. She also gave me a card that said although she understood that I might be tempted to stray, with all of my travel and time spent away from home, she would be there patiently waiting . . . to separate me from my testicles should I choose to do so. So far, there is no conclusive evidence that she was kidding about either.

2. Jim Collins and Morten T. Hansen, *Great By Choice* (New York: HarperCollins, 2011), 29.

3. Mark Ellwood, "Time Priorities for Top Managers." Paper presented to the International Association of Time Use Researchers (ATUR) Conference, Halifax, November 2005, www.paceproductivity.com/files/Time_Priorities_for_Top_Managers.pdf.

CHAPTER 9   GENERATE CREATIVE TENSION

1. Daryl R. Conner, *Managing at the Speed of Change* (New York: Villard Books, 1993).

2. Diana Hughes, M.D., "Psychiatric Aspects of Heart Disease," www.longislandpsych.org/articles/archive/heart.cfm.

3. Edward E. Whitacre, Jr., and Leslie Cauley, "How Ed Whitacre Brought GM Back from the Brink," *Fortune* (February 4, 2013).

CHAPTER 10 CONNECT WITH PEOPLE WHERE THEY ARE

1. Scott Keller and Carolyn Aiken, "The Inconvenient Truth about Change Management," www.mckinsey.com/App_Media/Reports/ Financial_Services/The_Inconvenient_Truth_About_Change_ Management.pdf.

2. Dan Ariely, *Predictably Irrational,* revised and expanded edition (New York: Harper Perennial, 2009), 2.

3. Joe Malarkey is really my good friend George Campbell. Check him out at www.JoeMalarkey.com.

CHAPTER 11 INVOLVE EARLY AND OFTEN

1. IBM Global Business Services Strategy & Change Practice, "Making Change Work," 2008, www-935.ibm.com/services/us/ gbs/bus/pdf/gbe03100-usen-03-making-change-work.pdf.

2. "Coke Lore: New Coke," November 14, 2012, www.coca -colacompany.com/stories/coke-lore-new-coke.

CHAPTER 13 WHEN CHANGE ISN'T A CHOICE

1. I have been fortunate to have many excellent managers and supervisors, but with all due respect to them, Bill taught me more about how great supervisors treat people than any others.

2. Bruce Schoenfeld, "The Art of Rebounding," *Men's Health* 18, no. 1 (January/February 2003).

3. Ibid.

CHAPTER 14 CHANGE YOUR CULTURE AND CHANGE YOUR RESULTS

1. Bryan Mahoney, "USAA—A Study in Pervasive Innovation," November 16, 2012, www.innovationexcellence.com/blog/ 2012/11/16/usaa-a-study-in-pervasive-innovation/.

2. Ben D. Gardner Sood, "Busting the 21 Days Habit Formation Myth," *Health Chatter: The Health Behaviour Research Centre Blog,* June 29, 2012, http://blogs.ucl.ac.uk/hbrc/2012/06/29/ busting-the-21-days-habit-formation-myth/.

CHAPTER 15   STOP SPINEATING

1. Randy Pennington, *Results Rule!* (Hoboken, NJ: Wiley, 2006), 48.

CHAPTER 16   THE FUTURE AND CHANGE

1. IBM Global Technology Services, "The Toxic Terabyte: How Data-Dumping Threatens Business Efficiency," Contributors: Paul Coles, Tony Cox, Chris Mackey, and Simon Richardson, July 2006, www-935.ibm.com/services/no/cio/leverage/levinfo_wp_gts_thetoxic.pdf.

2. "Congress Approval Ties All-Time Low at 10%," Gallup Politics, August 14, 2012, www.gallup.com/poll/156662/congress-approval-ties-time-low.aspx.

3. "United States Congressional Elections Results, 2012," BallotPedia, http://ballotpedia.org/wiki/index.php/United_States_Congressional_elections_results,_2012#tab=US_House_analysis.

4. Daniel Burrus with John David Mann, *Flash Foresight: How to See the Invisible and Do the Impossible* (New York: Harper Business, 2011).

5. Mary Madden, Amanda Lenhart, Maeve Duggan, Sandra Cortesi, and Urs Gasser, "Teens and Technology 2013," Pew Internet and American Life Project, March 13, 2013, www.pewinternet.org/Reports/2013/Teens-and-Tech.aspx.

6. Amanda Lenhar, "Teens & Online Video," Pew Internet and American Life Project, May 3, 2012, pewinternet.org/Reports/2012/Teens-and-online-video/Findings.aspx.

7. Linda A. Jacobsen, Mary Kent, Marlene Lee, and Mark Mather, "America's Aging Population," *Population Reference Bureau* 66, no. 1 (February 2011), www.prb.org/Publications/Population Bulletins/2011/americas-aging-population.aspx?p=1.

8. Janet Lowe, *Jack Welch Speaks: Wisdom from the World's Greatest Business Leader* (New York: John Wiley & Sons, 1998). *Note:* You saw the first portion of this quote in the Preface of this book. The entire quote is included here by design.

ABOUT THE AUTHOR

Randy Pennington is a resource for leaders who expect results. He is author of three books including the award-winning *Results Rule! Build a Culture that Blows the Competition Away.*

Randy presents to and consults with organizations that want to create a culture committed to results, relationships, and accountability. His clients include leading companies, government agencies, and institutions of higher education. For information regarding presentations, seminars, leadership retreats, consulting services, change guidance, and coaching please contact:

Pennington Performance Group
4004 Winter Park Lane
Addison, Texas 75001
972.980.9857 (US)
www.penningtongroup.com
www.penningtongroup.com/make-change-work/

CONNECT WITH RANDY

 www.Twitter.com/RandyPennington

 www.Facebook.com/RandyGPennington

 www.YouTube.com/RandyGPennington

 www.linkedin.com

INDEX

Ability:
   to adapt, 36
   to change, 29
Abuse, of crisis, **80**
Accountability, 27
   courage of, 133
   ensuring, 48, 49
Action:
   crisis and, **79**
   empowering, 49
Action list, 9–11, 19–20, 31–32,
      39–40, 50, 57, 65, 72–74,
      82–83, 93, 102, 111–112,
      124, 133
Adaptability:
   to change, 29–30, 69
   coyote as model for, 37–38
Affordable Care Act/ObamaCare,
      24, 25
AFP. *See* Another Fine Program
      (AFP)
Aiken, Carolyn, 88, 90
Alignment:
   of efforts, 91
   of process, structure, and
      systems, 49
Ambiguity, tolerating, 63
American Airlines, 107
Another Fine Program (AFP),
      71–72
Answers, in proportion to
      questions, 20
Anxiety:
   change and, 9
   long-term, confidence and, 10

Apathy, benign, 55
Apple, **80**
Arab Spring, 12, 25
Argumentative individual, 110
Ariely, Dan, 89
Assessment, of current
      culture, 133
Assignments, related to
      change, 110
Assumptions, habits and, 132
Attitude, bad, 110
Awareness, 98, 100, 132

Banking crisis, of 2008, 7
Bankruptcy, General Motors and,
      81–82
Baxter (Rethink Robotics), 18
Becoming a Category of One
      (Calloway), 16
Behaviors, consistent, 64–65
Beliefs, habits and, 132
Benign apathy, 55
Bonaparte, Napoleon, 123
Brain, left and right, 46–47
Bridges, William, 30
BSC. *See* Business Service
      Center (BSC)
Burning platform, **78, 79**
Burrus, Daniel, 148
Business, role of technology in, 6
Business Service Center (BSC),
      53–54, 56–57
Buy-in, 28
   about, 55
   absence of, 55

Buy-in (*continued*)
  achieving, 131–132
  building and sustaining for
    change, 56, 141
  for change, 98
  generating, 99
  new culture and building, 130
  occurrence of, 55–56
  participation, collaboration,
    empowerment, and, 99
  trust and, 93
  vision and, 55

Calloway, Joe, 15
Campbell, George, 91
Capacity, building, 48, 49
Carrollton, Texas, 18–19
Challenge(s):
  of cultural change, 129–130
  of implementing changes, 111
  of involvement, 99
  organizational spineating as,
    138–139
  recognizing, 120
  support and, 57
Change. *See also* Failure of; Good
    change; Successful change
  getting better at, 31–32
  large-scale, 99
  negative connotation of, 72
  reasons for, 77–78
  test for evaluating, 23–24
  three parts of, 30
  Wright, Quincy, about, 7
Change agents, crisis and, 82
Change leader action list, 9–11,
    19–20, 31–32, 39–40, 50, 57,
    65, 72–74, 82–83, 93, 102,
    111–112, 124, 133
Change leadership:
  goals and, 47
  importance of, 46
  as right-brained activity, 47
  as skill and art, 50
  tasks of, 47–49

Change management:
  focusing on, 31
  goals and, 47
  as left-brained activity, 47
  plan, 45
  role of, 46
Change process:
  awareness and, 98
  influence in, 25
  perception and, 29
Circumstances, managing, 106
Clients. *See* Customers
Collaboration, 98, 99
Comfort zone, change and
    pushing out of, 56
Commitment:
  to awareness, change effort
    and, 100
  change and, 27
Communication:
  during crisis, 83
  delivering messages,
    121–122
  effective, 93
  lack of, change and, 28
  plan for, 124
  resistance and, 108
  technology and, 8
Company(ies). *See also*
    Organization(s)
  Great Depression and, 11
  timid, 10
  using tools, 17
Competencies, building and
    maintaining, 132
Competitive advantage, change
    as, xviii
Compliance, mandating, 64
Concerns, discussing, 110
Confidence:
  facing crisis requiring change
    and, 83
  in the future, 118
  lack of, 10–11
  trust and, 92

Conner, Daryl, **78**
Connor, John, 18
Consequences, positive, 73–74
Control, 100, 101–102,
    119, 122
Coping, change and, 25–26
Corporate-speak, interpretation
    of, 91
Cost:
    change and, 30
    of change *vs.* staying the
        same, 25
Cost containment, 149
Coyote:
    embracing, 150
    in praise of, 37–38
Creative tension, creating, 77–83
Credibility:
    increasing, 124
    of managers, change and, 25
Crisis:
    abuse of, **80**
    change agents and, 82
    change and, 77–78
    communicating during, 83
    message about, 87
    renewed focus and, **79–80**
    urgency and, **79, 80**
Crystal, Billy, 65
Culture:
    building, 127
    change, challenge of, 129–130
    defined, 128–129
    leveraging partnerships, 26
    new, creating, 130–131
    in organizations, 129
    program for changing, 131–132
    strategy and, 127–128
Customers:
    defining expectations, 19
    evaluating services, 16–17
    expectation of, 148
    listening to, 15
    questions about experiences
        of, 16

Decision(s):
    to change, 77
    leaders and supporting of,
        121, 122
    public support for, 122
Democracy, rise in Arab Spring of
    2012, 23
Dodo, 150
    in defense of, 35–36
    factors leading to the demise
        of, 36
DSW Shoes, 130
Dutch Tulip Bubble of 1637, 7

Economics, technology and, 8
Economy, growth of, 5
Effort:
    recognizing, 83
    undermining, 107
Ellwood, Mark, 71
Emanuel, Rahm, **78, 79**
Emotional readiness, 29, 77
Emotion(s):
    lowering, 122
    resistance and, 105
    separating response from, 119
Employees:
    adding value for the
        investment, 10
    involvement of, 97–99
Employee survey, 61
Employers, relevancy and value of
        employees, 10
Employment, terminating,
    122–123
Empowerment, 98, 99
    belief in, 101
    control and, 100, 101–102
Ending/old way, change and, 30
Engagement, change and, 27
Environment:
    adapting to change in, 69
    changing, 35–36
    hyper-change, thriving in, 9
European sovereign debt crisis, 23

Evaluation:
  of change, tests for, 23–24
  of change efforts, 23, 57
  of efforts, customers and, 16–17
  against experience, 19
  of responses to change, 24–26
  of success, 27, 64
Expectations:
  customer, 148
  of customers, meeting, 15
  customers and defining, 19
  disrupted, adapting to change
    and, 29–30
Experience:
  customers, evaluation through,
    19–20
  past, influence of, 29
  questions about, 16

Facts, focus on, 121
Failure of change:
  blaming for, 64
  reasons for, 27–28
Feedback:
  about behavior, 110
  providing, 83, 110
Feeling, thinking and, 118, 124
Focus:
  on change management, 31
  facts on, 121
  on process, leadership and, 31
  renewing, **79–80**
  on value given and received, 10
  on what you know, 148
Functioning, change and, 25–26
Future:
  creating expectations of, 122
  exploring, 120
  investing in, 10
  present guided by, 71
  trends driving success in, 148–149
  uncertainty about, 5

Gallup organization, 147
General Motors, 81–82

Gerstner, Louis, Jr., 131
Globalization:
  opportunities and threats of,
    6–7
  technology and, 8
Goals, 27
  creating, 64
  change and, 25
  change leadership and, 47
  change management and, 47
  establishing, 49
  leaders and supporting organiza-
    tion's, 121
  measurable, establishing, 48
Going first:
  to build realistic optimists, 63
  setting the example of, 64
  seven behaviors of, 63–64
Goizueta, Roberto, 100
Good change, 26–27
Google, 129
Great Depression of 1930s, 11
Gretzky, Wayne, 70
Group favorite, 111
Group membership, assimilating
    and strengthening,
    132
Grudge carrier, 111
Guidelines, change and, 28
Guilfoy, Tom, 19

Habit(s):
  culture and, 132
  formation of, 131
  in organizations, breaking spine-
    ating, 140
Hard work, Crystal about change
    as, 65
Help, offering, 122
Henderson, Fritz, 81–82
Henry, John, 6
Hope:
  during crisis, providing, 83
  for the future, 82
Hughes, Diana, 80

Hyper-change environment, people in, 9

IBM Global Business Services Strategy & Change Practice, 97
IBM Global Technology Services, 147
Idea(s). *See also* Idea(s), new
  implementation of, 111
  people and, 97, 112
  resistors and, 108
  sharing, 110
Idea(s), new:
  change and reinforcing, 73
  openness to, 64
If The Government Gets It, Why Doesn't Everyone? (Case study), 18–19
Influence:
  in change process, 25
  of past experience, 29
  personal performance and, 65
Initiatives, 28, 32
Innovations:
  opportunity and change with, **80–81**
  at USAA, 128
Input, 98, 100
Instability:
  change and, 9
  confidence and, 10
Intel, 8
Intellectual understanding, 29
Involvement:
  challenge of, 99
  of employees, 97–99
Iron Lady. *See* Thatcher, Lady Margaret
IT Shared Services (ITSS), 54, 56–57
ITSS. *See* IT Shared Services (ITSS)

Job market, 5
Johnson, Dave, 119
Jonathan Livingston Seagull, 35

Keller, Scott, 88, 90
King, Martin Luther, Jr., 56
Know-it-alls, 110
Knowledge capacity, 49

Language:
  of continuous improvement, 72
  of success, cultivating, 132
Large-scale change, 99
Leaders. *See also* Leadership
  of BSC and ITSS, 56–57
  building culture and, 127
  building realistic optimists and, 63
  change and, 28
  credibility of, change and, 92
  as motivators for change, 81
  role of, 90
  setting the example of going first, 64
  seven behaviors of, 63–64
  supporting organization's goals, 121
Leadership. *See also* Change leadership
  Bonaparte on, 123
  focus on process, 31
  of ITSS, messages of, 54
  participation and, 98
  as skill and art, 50
  trust in, 56
Leading change, 100
Left-brainers, 46–48
Legends, leveraging, 132
Les Schwab Tire Centers, 129
Level of work, value and recognizing, 64
Lewin, Kurt, 30
Lincoln, Abraham, 56

Listening, 122
  to customers, 15
  to feelings, 118
  to reason, resistor and, 106
Long-range planning, tracking
    time in, 71

Malarkey, Joe, 91
Management By Best Seller
    (MBBS), 71–72
Managing at the Speed of Change
    (Conner), **78**
Markets, stable, returning to, 5
Martin, Leonard, 19, 106–107
MBBS. *See* Management By Best
    Seller (MBBS)
Messages, tips for formulating,
    121–122
Metrics:
  establishing, 49
  to evaluate success, 27
Mind-set, changing, 57
Mission, linking change leadership
    to, 48
Mobile digital technology, 23
Money magazine, 18
Moore, Gordon, 8
Moore's Law, 8, 9
Mortgage crisis, of 2008, 7
Moses, Anna Mary Robertson,
    120, 124
Motivation, 77, 81, 91

Network (movie), 105
New beginning, change and, 30
New Coke, 100
Next change, moving to, 28
Nimbleness, coyote as model for,
    37–38
Nordstrom, 129
Normalcy, return to, 5
Norville, Deborah, 120

Obedience, malicious, 55
O'Brien, Dan, 119–120

Obsolete, becoming, 69
Occupy movement, 106
Open questioning, 55
Opportunity(ies):
  change and, 77
  change as, 72, 74
  change with innovations and,
    80–81
  for involving people, 102
  looking for, 37
  message about, 87
Optimists, realistic and unrealistic,
    62, 63
Organizational structure,
    employee survey into, 61
Organization(s):
  agile, difficulty to be, 29
  big changes and, 8
  breaking spineating habit in,
    140
  change and people in, 61
  culture and, 127, 129
  demise of dodo and, 36
  leaders and support of, 121,
    122
  reason for change, 77–78
  successful, change in,
    26–27

P. R. Inc., 16
Pace Productivity Inc., 71
Participation, 98, 99, 100
Partnerships, 26, 38, 98
Pennington, Jack, 118
People:
  change and, 8, 63
  connecting to, 91
  connecting with, 88
  in hyper-change environment, 9
  nimble, difficulty to be, 29
  pulling ideas out of, 112
  reason for change, 77
  successful change and, 97
  timid, 10
  ways of reacting to change, 62

Perception(s):
  of change, changing, 72–74
  change process and, 29
  past, 119, 139
  unrealistic, change and, 63
Performance, 129
  level of, 19, 70
  past and future, 119
  personal, influence and, 65
Perot, Ross, xviii
Personal performance, influence
    and, 65
Pessimists, realistic and
    unrealistic, 62
Pew Research Center, 148
Planning and preparation, resis-
    tance and, 111
Policy, change and, 24
Politicians, burning platforms
    and, **78**
Power, use of, 106
Procedure, aligning, 132
Process(es):
  alignment of structure, system,
    and, 49, 132
  change and, 28
  leadership and focus on, 31
Procter & Gamble, 130
Publix, 129
Purpose, 27, 132

Questioning, open, 55
Questions:
  about customers' experiences, 16
  about resistance, 110
  beyond status quo, asking, 20
  on change efforts and initiatives,
    31–32
  on feelings, 110

Reaction, to change, 62
Reagan, Ronald, 109
Realistic optimists:
  change and support of, 63
  creating, 62

Realistic pessimists, 62
Reality:
  acknowledging, 119
  current, defining, 132
Reasoning, use of, 106–107
Relationships, trust and, 82, 93
Relevancy, threat of, 10, 90
Resilience, culture and, 128
Resistance:
  benefits of, 107
  to change, dealing with, 106
  to derail change, 28
  guerilla, 107
  one-to-one conversation, 110
  overcoming, 109
  pushing back against, 109
  reasonable people and, 107
  stepping up, 106
  treating with respect, 108
  types of, 109–111
Resistors:
  ignoring, 106
  listening to reason, 106–107
  reasonable, 107
Resource allocation, 27
Resource capacity, 49
Responsibility, 119
  determining, 124
  for perceptions, 118
Results:
  change and, 25, 26
  culture and, 127–133
  delivering, 15, 20
  not defined, change and, 27
Results Rule! (Pennington), 26,
    140
Rethink Robotics, 18
Return on investment, 10
Right-brainers, 47–48
Road Runner cartoons, 37

Sabotage (overt or covert), 55
Sense of urgency, building, 48
September 11, 2001, perspective of
    Lady Thatcher about, 6

Sewell's Lexus and Cadillac
    dealership, 140
Shy clam individuals, 110
Skeptic individuals, 111
Skills capacity, 49
Social media, 8, 23, 24, 25
Southwest Airlines, 127, 129
Spence, Bill, 117, 124
Strategy, culture and, 127–128
Structure, alignment of process,
    system, and, 49, 132
Success, 91, 92
    blaming for, 64
    celebrating, 120
    of change, 97
    evaluating, 64
    language of, cultivating, 132
Successful change:
    evaluating, 26
    factors of, 50
    leadership strategies for, 57
    people and, 97
    truths about, 149–150
Support:
    bargaining for, 106
    building, 48, 49
    challenges and, 57
    change and enhancing, 57
    change and level of, 92
    of organizations, leaders and,
        121, 122
    public, for decision, 122
Symbols, leveraging, 132

Talent:
    culture and, 128
    keeping best and brightest,
        148
Team(s):
    assessment
    change for, 65
    implementation of new policy
        for, 23
    interpretation of corporate-
        speak, 91–92

perception, changing, 71
    setting up, rules of, 100
Team work, 38
Tea Party movement, 106
Technology:
    globalization and, 9
    Moore's Law and, 8
    role in life and work, 6
Teerlink, Richard, 71–72
Tension, creative, 82, 83
Test:
    for evaluating change, 23–24
    time, 70–71, 74
Thatcher, Lady Margaret, 6, 56
Thinking, feeling and, 118, 124
Thomas, Carl, 16
3D vision, 63, 64
Time test, 70–71, 74
Transition period, change and, 30
Trust:
    in leadership, 56
    partnerships and, 26
    relationships and, 82, 93
Truth:
    acknowledging, 122
    facing crisis requiring change
        and, 83

Uncertainty, about future, 5
Universal principle, 77
University College London, 131
University of North Texas (UNT)
    System. See UNT System
Unrealistic optimists, 62
Unrealistic pessimists, 62
UNT System:
    initial planning to implementa-
        tion, 56–57
    kickoff of organizational struc-
        ture, 53–54
UNT System IT Shared Services
    (ITSS), 54
Urgency:
    bankruptcy of General Motors
        and, 81–82

building, 48
crisis and, **79, 80**
maintaining, 49
USAA, 128, 129

Value(s):
change and adding, 25
defining, 132
focus on, 10
habits and, 132
linking change leadership to, 48
Vision, 38
buy-in and, 55
defining, 132
3D, 63
linking change leadership
to, 48
for success, 83

Wall St. Journal, **78**
Wars, technology and, 8

Welch, Jack, 149
Whitacre, Ed, Jr., 81–82
Whole Foods, 130
Work:
accomplishment, change and, 8
impact of technology on, 8
level of, value and recognizing,
64
Working alone (Coyotes), 38
World:
impact of technology on
the, 8
Lady Thatcher perspective
about, 6
as unstable place, 7
Wright, Quincy, 7

YouTube, 147

Zappos, 129
Ziglar, Zig, 77